Our Animal Brothers

You, the Animal—You, the Human

Who Has Higher Values?

Life with
Our Animal Brothers and Sisters

You, the Animal –
You, the Human Being

Who Has Higher Values?

Liobani,
a pure spirit being from the heavens,
gives a revelation
through the prophetess of God in our time,
Gabriele – Würzburg

Verlag DAS WORT GmbH
THE UNIVERSAL SPIRIT
LIVING IN THE SPIRIT OF GOD

First Edition, 2003
Published by:

Gabriele Publishing House
P.O. Box 2221, Deering, NH 03244
(844) 576-0937
WhatsApp/Messenger: +49 151 1883 8742
www.Gabriele-Publishing-House.com

Licensed edition
translated from the original German title:
Du, das Tier – Du, der Mensch
Order No. S 133en

From the Universal Life Series
with the consent of
© Verlag DAS WORT GmbH
im Universellen Leben
Max-Braun-Str. 2
97828 Marktheidenfeld/Altfeld, Germany

The German edition is the work of reference for all
questions regarding the meaning of the contents

ISBN 1-890841-25-0

Table of Contents

I Am Everything in All Things

The All-Holy One speaks:
I Am the Eternal One and the Eternal. I Am
the Creator, the beginning of creation and the
creation itself, which is eternal.

Without Me, the great All-One, there is nei-
ther life nor life forms, for I Am the life and
the substance of life and the power in all forms
of life.
I Am everything in all things.
I Am the Creator of the universes, of all suns
and stars.
I Am the Father of all divine beings, of all men
and souls.
The Being, the pure, Am I, the Creator, and
the Father-Mother-God.
I am everything in all things.
Whatever has taken and takes on form in the
eternal Being is, in turn, Me, the substance
and the power—the life.
There is no nothing. Everything is power, life
and the substance of life.

I Am the Eternal and the eternity—
from eternity to eternity,
from eon to eon.

My word is the word of all pure beings, the word of true inspiration

I have already introduced myself with the name Liobani to my human brothers and sisters in the teachings and instructions for life directed toward children and young people.

My brothers and sisters in the earthly garment now receive the holy, eternal word, the Being, in my revelation "You, the Animal—You, the Human. Who Has Higher Values?"

I am a spirit being in the light of eternity. My light-name, which is in the Eternal and which was breathed into me by the Eternal, cannot be conveyed with human words on the Earth, for the light-names of all divine beings and of all spiritual life forms are infinitely eternal, pure cosmic law.

The eternal Being is perfection; it is Absolute Law. All light-names—of the spirit beings, of the minerals, plants, animals and nature beings—are aspects of the Absolute Law, because these life forms are from God and in God, and live and have their existence in the mighty stream of the All.

People with spiritual knowledge also call their divine brothers and sisters angels; many are teaching angels. I, Liobani, also live in the stream of the eternal Being and teach according to my spiritual mentality and my spiritual abilities as a teaching angel in the spiritual planes of development. I instruct the spiritual children, also called angel children, on how to apply the eternal cosmic law in a lawful way.

The emergence of humans and of the Earth: The reversal process from the pure spiritual, the fine material, to the coarse material

The spiritual body which, burdened and incarnated, is called a soul lives on theEarth in an envelopment that we call the human being. Not until the soul has been purified of its burdens, that is, liberated, does it become a pure being again. Then, as the All that has spiritually taken on form, it lives again consciously in the All-stream, God, from which the spiritual divine body, the pure being, went forth.

The All-stream is the eternal divine law that flows through infinity. It flows through all forms of Being, all divine beings, all pure heavens with their planets and divine nature kingdoms. It also flows through the planes of preparation, the planes of unfoldment, which group around the pure Being and on which the purified souls prepare for their return home into the eternal Being. The eternal law also flows through and maintains the purification planes and the souls which live there in order to purify themselves. The eternal law also flows through and maintains part-matter— and matter with its stars and the Earth with its people and nature kingdoms.

All spiritual forms came and come forth from the great All-One.

He is the breath of the All and the All itself. He, the All-One, spoke His almighty word, and the first beings and life forms emerged.

All pure beings and life forms are the All that has taken on form. The All-law flows in them. They are substance and power of the All. Through the Creator, the All-Spirit, who is at the same time the principle of creation, everything is contained in all things.

The Earth with its people has the rhythm of day and night and the hours, minutes, seconds and moments. People call this rhythm "time." If they do not live consciously in the day, then they are lived by the day and its events; this is why only few pay attention to the eternal laws of God and why they often see themselves as soul-less—as "only human."

The human body is merely the protective shell for the soul that dwells in it, for the spiritual body. The material of this shell consists of matter. In this materiality, the soul can live on matter, on the Earth, in order to clear up in the brevity of years what it inflicted on itself in previous incarnations—and perhaps even in this incarnation.

The protective shell, the human, emerged very gradually. To the degree to which the emerging human being rebelled against the eternal law, the spiritual body enveloped itself in materiality, in the vibrations that the human being sent out —and which came back to him according to the law of "sowing and reaping." Over the course of the ages, the material garment, the protective shell, became ever denser, and its vibrations became increasingly coarse. What very gradually crystallized out of this was and is the human being.

The beings that had turned away from God—also called Fall-beings—and burdened themselves more and more, fell into ever deeper zones of the All. With them, parts of pure spiritual planets also fell, which, similar to the Fall-beings, enveloped themselves in coarse matter.

As a result of the Fall-event, the planes of preparation and of purification developed, and the coarse material developed, which, in its state of greatest density, is called matter. In human terms, this reversal process from the fine-material to the coarse-material took countless epochs of time.

As it is in heaven, it is similar on Earth.

The heavenly planets carry the spiritual nature kingdoms—the Earth carries the condensed nature kingdoms.

The spiritual nature kingdoms consist of minerals, plants and animals of all kinds, similar to the nature kingdoms of the Earth; the nature beings, too, are a part of them. The part-planets, which slipped from the eternal Being as a result of the Fall, carried spiritual minerals, spiritual plants and animals, which gradually condensed and became coarse-material, that is, matter.

Everything that vibrates and moves outside the pure Being is enveloped in a corresponding rate of vibration. And so, anything that is not pure primordial substance bears a magnetic shell, which can be called a mantle. A person, too, moves in his self-made magnetic shell. According to the law of sowing and reaping, he attracts what he sends out; for what he sows, that is, what he sends out, is what he reaps, what he receives.

No energy is lost: Whatever negative energy the individual Fall-being sent out fell back onto the Fall-being; it enveloped itself with this. At the same time, it contributed to the envelopment of the spiritual part-planets.

Over the course of becoming human, the shells condensed more and more, through which the material body and the material universe emerged.

Many people are of the opinion that from generation to generation different people come into this world. It only seems this way, however, because the souls appear again and again in different shells—in different physical bodies—that correspond only indirectly to the previously discarded shell. The characteristics that the soul radiates when incarnating again mark the physical garment; with this, the soul forms its shell, the human being. The soul, which is fully incarnated only upon its actual birth, forms itself already in the womb, in the embryonic state, that is, in the already developing human body.

The Soul—
The book of life on Earth

The person, the shell, bears in itself the soul and in the soul, the incorruptible core of being, the spark of the Spirit, God. For this reason, the human being consists of spirit, soul and body.

Whatever a person senses, thinks, speaks and how he acts enters his soul, which has become the book of his life on Earth. What the soul has absorbed into its soul-particles radiates out, in turn, via the person. The soul of a person is therefore called the book of his deeds, of his sensing, thinking, speaking and acting. Whatever goes out from a person, both the divine as well as the un-divine, enters him again. This marks his character and his external shell.

And so, both the divine as well as the un-divine is registered by the soul in its spiritual particles and is then radiated out again. With its magnetic radiation, the soul also takes up contact with the radiation of planets and perhaps with the forces that are active there, for example, energy fields or souls that resemble the radiation of the soul and the person.

The spiritual law says: Like attracts like. What the soul radiates via its shell, the human being, is registered by the corresponding planet radiation. After the passing of the physical body, the shell of the soul, the soul is then attracted by that planet which corresponds to its present radiation.

According to its radiation, every soul is registered in the All several times. During its journey to perfection, the soul is attracted over and over again by the radiation of those planets that correspond to its frequency of vibration—in order to meet up with souls that live there and with which it needs to clear up things, as do the souls with it. In the soul realms or as a human being living on Earth, the soul will expiate those causes that are registered in the soul's particles to the extent to which the corresponding effects come toward the soul or the person according to the law of sowing and reaping.

The soul thus has several options for expiating its guilt: either as a human being in the brevity of years or as a soul in the soul realms—perhaps there in long cycles—or in alternation with further incarnations.

And so, what a person senses, thinks, speaks and how he acts, including his passions and longings, his driving desires, his possessive claims in what he wants to be and to have—all this is registered in the particles of his soul and also in the radiation of the corresponding planets. Everything is vibration. How the individual person acts in relation to the laws of inner life—either for or against God—so is his radiation, so is his vibration. According to this, he is also in communication with the forces of the All.

What the soul or the person has not yet cleared up remains registered in the radiation of the respective planets, until it is paid off—either by the soul in the purification planes or by the human being. Many souls that lived on Earth in previous incarnations, and that live at present as people on Earth again, or that will come back and have not yet cleared up their causes, remain registered in the Fall-planets—until they repent of their negativities, ask for forgiveness, forgive and no longer commit the faults they have recognized.

Every soul, no matter which level it is on, wears the garment—that is, the envelopment—of its deeds. What the soul brings with it into this side of life—its sins from previous incarnations that it has not yet atoned for or light-filled, divine aspects—this is what the soul, in turn, radiates. The soul's garment corresponds to the frequencies of that planet on which it lives. The same is true for people. The structure of the physical body corresponds to what the soul bears within, light or shadow. According to the spiritual law "like attracts like," people attract those people who have similar vibrations, who think, speak and act in a similar way. Like-minded people thus always attract like-minded people.

The light or the shadows of the soul form the human body. The way a person radiates, so is his behavior toward his environment, so is his conduct, his gestures and his facial expressions, so is his thinking, speaking and acting. With this, the person and soul identify themselves and give evidence about who they are—whether they are aware of this or not. Every person is thus an open book that a person of sincere heart is able to read.

Every soul is in God—whether it lives without a body on that purification planet that corresponds to its rate of vibration, or whether it lives in a body as a human being on Earth, the place of probation and expiation—because the incorruptible part of the soul, the divine, has its existence in the stream of God. On the other hand, the envelopment of the soul, the person, who is of the Earth, is given back to the Earth after the death of the body.

God calls people to use the power of Christ to clear up those causes that were brought by the soul into the body as well as those causes that the person inflicted upon his soul during the course of his earthly existence. In this way, the soul may purify and ennoble itself and is able to return into the stream of God as a divine being. During the journey of the embodied soul toward the divine, the structure of the person also becomes finer, so that soul and person attain higher rates of vibration, and things also go better for the person day by day.

The purpose of a life on Earth is for the soul in a human being to purify itself in the brevity of its existence on Earth, in order to return into God's light, from where the spirit being went out. Whatever changes in the soul from the negative to the lawful, to the positive, is erased from the stars and planets of the purification planes, which are also called repository planets.

The path of unfoldment of the spiritual life forms, from a spiritual atom via the steps of evolution to a perfect spirit being

God is the eternal All-Being, the All- law. God is Father, Mother and Creator. He is the Father and the Mother of His children—and the Creator-God of all life forms, of the minerals, plants, animals and of the nature beings, which are in evolution toward the filiation of God. God is freedom. This is why already at the beginning of the "Let there be," of the all-encompassing spiritual event of creation, the Eternal breathed free will into the life that was in formation. By constantly breathing the All-law in and out, the Eternal guides all life forms to perfection, all the way to the fully developed spirit being.

Every life form that gradually develops into a nature being starts its journey of becoming as one of the spiritual atoms fertilized by the All-radiation in the developing spiritual particle. God, the Eternal, breathes the evolution toward the filiation of God into a spiritual atom which is intended for spiritual formation.

All predispositions for becoming a spirit being are already contained in the first ray of the "Let there be," the corresponding mentality and the abilities of the spirit being and its heavenly name as well. Everything is absolute and therefore everything is consistent with each other, the mentality and the abilities. Mentality and abilities are consistent with the spiritual name, and the spiritual name with the abilities and the mentality. What God creates is perfect; it is absolute harmony in sound, color, form and fragrance.

Through the constant breathing in and out of the All-Law, further atoms and spiritual particles are created, which at first take their place in collectives. Out of these, the spiritual body then evolves very gradually.

And so, the spiritual body in formation consists of spiritual particles. When the life form is completed, then it is the spirit being, the All that has taken on form.

The spiritual life forms of the different levels of development, which are also different levels of consciousness, up to the perfect spirit being have neither cells nor organs. Only the material body consists of bones, tissues and other material organs with specific functions. This makes it possible for the soul to live on Earth. The earthly shell, the person, is oriented toward the Earth. The pure spirit being, however, is All-conscious. For the All that has taken on form, the spirit being, there are no limitations: it is All-conscious.

Because of the constant breathing in and out of the Creator-God, through which light and energy radiate into the All without interruption, the spiritual body gradually unfolds via divine spectral lights during cycles of eons.

First, the predispositions develop to form a spiritual collective for minerals. Only then does a mineral take on form. Each form of development must absorb all the energies for the developing awareness of its respective level of evolution. And so, the mineral first absorbs all the energies for the developing awareness of the mineral kingdoms, whereby always different spectra of light become effective. Thus, many evolutionary steps are needed until a spiritual mineral has emerged and fully matured. Then, in cycles of further eons, the next evolutionary step builds up.

From the human point of view, it is a long and slow path of unfoldment until a spiritual life form is built up and completed.

Without comprehending the value of a mineral, for example, of a stone, a person speaks disdainfully, often pejoratively, about minerals and stones. In reality, every mineral, every stone, is something quite special. The mineral, the stone, already radiates its intensity, its nature. It radiates what the Creator- God breathed into the first spiritual atom, out of which the life form develops.

Because everything is consciousness, every life form has its state of consciousness. The state of consciousness of a life form is the developed consciousness of the life form, which radiates the predispositions—like the mentality, the abilities and the consciousness-name—which were breathed into it by the Creator-God, all according to the state of consciousness of this life form. Human beings give names to minerals, stones, plants and animals. But these do not correspond to the consciousness-name that the Eternal breathed into the emerging life form.

Many people focus only on the external, and therefore perceive only external forms and colors. According to their state of consciousness, they then describe what shows itself to them in the material world, for example, the minerals, plants and animals. Just as a person sees and classifies the life forms, as he estimates their usefulness to him, so will he give them a value and name. As long as a person looks only to the exterior, he cannot comprehend the values of the inner being nor those of the life forms. For an externalized person, the mineral, the stone, the plant and the animal remain objects without life-feelings and, so he thinks, can be treated according to his externalized world of thoughts.

As long as a person looks only at the shell of Being, he does not grasp the life in all its forms, nor does he show any understanding for the life that does not have his form. Only when a person becomes conscious of the filiation of God, will he gain access to the cosmic laws, to the forces in the forms of life on Earth. From this, understanding and the capacity to empathize grow.

By unfolding his inner values, a person gradually gains access to the divine Being, which is effective in all life forms, and he also regains communication with all the forms of the All. During this spiritual process of development of his divine consciousness, which refrains from externalization, from the human ego, he begins to sense and to understand the eternal life, the Being, in everything, no matter how it shows itself. During this maturing process of the soul in the divine, the person feels more and more in his inner being the fine vibrations, which all forms of life emit. It is only then that he understands that every life form communicates, that is, manifests itself, according to its state of consciousness.

For a spiritually developed person, the difficulty is to express the divine vibrations, the impulses, with his words, and this remains with him as long as he is a human being. According to his refined vocabulary, which also can express the impulses in only a limited way, he will convey them to his neighbor, but only if they are of importance for the latter. What the person has put into words is only a reflection of the pure, a pale shimmer—and not the impulse itself. Therefore, in the material world everything is relative, including the divine impulses that are conveyed with human words. They are terms and give indications; however, they are not the Absolute, the divine impulse, itself. For this reason, the reader should attempt to comprehend everything that is revealed out of the eternal Being according to its meaning, and not cling to the word, which is only a symbol and not the Absolute.

God, the Eternal, His Son, the Redeemer of all humans, and the spirit beings, to whom I, Liobani, also belong, speak to human beings through earthly instruments, that is, through people whose spiritual consciousness has been prepared for this, because the divine world, the heavenly Being, the All-power, the life, God, the stream of love in which we live, does not have the language of man. This is why the Eternal, His Son and the divine beings use the language of man in order to be understood by humans. In the divine revelations, the terms and vocabulary of the person whom God has made His instrument are used. Every term, every word, is thus relative. Therefore, the terms and words of revelation should be understood according to their meaning.

The human being is called upon to purify his soul in order to again grow closer to God, his eternal Father. This holds true solely for human beings, since their souls are burdened. In this way, the spiritual consciousness in the person unfolds again. The soul that dwells within him uncovers itself and becomes again what it once was: the pure, perfect spirit being, the All that has taken on form.

The spiritual development of all life forms up to the fully completed spirit being takes place exclusively in the spiritual development planes.

In the eternal Being there is nothing static; there are no boundaries—everything is flowing energy. What for people is the "here" and the "there" is for the spirit being the unity and the whole in itself.

Since in the pure Being everything is in all things, there is no here and there, no above and below, no right and left. Everything that exists is in every spirit being as current and energy, as picture and sound. In this cosmic principle, there is neither time nor space. Eternity is the Being in the children of the Being, the eternal, moving law, which is rhythm, form and sound of the All, in and on every spirit being. The eternal law, the rhythm of the All, consists of light cycles, also called eons. The evolution of the spiritual atom that has been stimulated by the Creator-God to form itself takes place in light cycles, from a particle to the fully completed spirit being. The spiritual body is therefore the compressed All, for it consists of all the forces of the All.

For humans who think in terms of time and space, the spiritual path of evolution all the way to the completion of the spirit being is an unimaginably long process of becoming.

When, over eons, that is, over light cycles, a nature form has developed to the point that it has become a fully matured nature being, then the next evolutionary step toward becoming the child takes place, which is the birth in the Father-Mother-Principle.

The spiritual body of a fully developed nature being, shortly before its evolutionary step into the filiation of God, carries within itself all substances in the All-Creation, from the mineral up to the full maturity of the nature being. According to its state of consciousness, the nature being will serve and help lawfully on the different steps of evolution that it has gone through in the mineral, plant and animal kingdoms.

The greatest evolutionary step is, as already revealed, the birth in the Father-Mother-Principle, which takes place through a dual-pair via spiritual procreation. The nature being is thus raised to the filiation of God by a dual-pair.

Recognize: No nature being is like another. Every nature being has developed the corresponding mentality and the particular abilities for a basic power of God. Mentality and abilities are in absolute harmony with one another. The predispositions of the fully developed nature being correspond, in turn, to the those of the dual-pair into which the nature being is spiritually born. When a nature being has been raised to filiation, then all divine predispositions already exist in it, including its absolute spiritual name, which, as already revealed, corresponds to the mentality and abilities of the spiritual child.

The image of God that the Creator-God breathed as a whole into a spiritual atom, that He led onto the path of unfoldment toward a perfect spirit being and that He accompanied on this path is then complete in the fully matured spirit being.

When nature beings have been raised to the filiation of God, then at the same time, via spiritual atoms that have been fertilized by the Creator-Spirit, new collectives build up again in the spiritual development planes from which new life forms come forth. The collectives—man also calls them group-souls—are respirated by the Creator-God and are guided to the next higher evolutionary level again and again.

Groups of minerals, plants and also of animals that do not yet have a part-soul, but which have similar predispositions, form a collective. When the life forms have reached a certain state of consciousness, then free will gradually unfolds in them. To the same extent that free will opens in a spiritual life form, so does this life form free itself from its collective, which then very gradually dissolves, since all the fully matured particles with similar predispositions form themselves into an independent body.

The life form, which is no longer bound to a collective, continues to mature by building up more and more particles, through which the spirit body completes itself. This takes place in a similar way as it does in the human body, which builds up by way of cells and tissues.

The more spiritual particles a life form consists of, the more flexible is the spiritual body. The development of the particles continues until the fully matured nature being is raised to be a spiritual child. Then it has developed in and on itself the forces of the All, which it, being a child of God, then learns to activate and to apply in all detail.

The spiritual particles, which through the evolutionary process very gradually join together to become a spiritual life form, carry in themselves countless spiritual atoms. The spiritual atoms contain the forces of the All as essence. They contain all energies of consciousness of the pure Being, of the stars, minerals, plants and animals. Every spiritual life form, including the completed spiritual body, consists solely of particles. The physical body, however, consists of bones, sinews and muscles—all in all, of cells. In its arrangement, the spiritual body corresponds to the structure of the whole creation, of the whole All.

When fully completed life forms of nature—man also calls them nature beings—are raised to filiation by a dual-pair, then they are spiritual children. In the spiritual development planes and in the spiritual worlds, the angel children are taught to activate all the forces of the All in their spiritual body, through which they establish a precise communication to all forms of life. In this way, the spiritual child continues to develop into a perfect spirit being.

The all-encompassing spiritual language, the spiritual primordial sensing— the absolute transmission in the direct vision

Although the spirit children bear within themselves all the seven basic powers of God, the law of the All, they have to grasp these again as a whole, by learning lawful communication—the sending and receiving—so that they are able to move freely within the whole of infinity. In the spiritual development planes, the spirit children also learn the all- encompassing spiritual language, the spiritual primordial sensing, which consists of innumerable sounds, colors and forms. In this way, they learn what the fully matured spirit beings have absolute command of: to see the messages of their neighbor within themselves as a complete picture.

Because all spirit beings bear within themselves the mentality and abilities of their neighbor as essence and power, they also receive within their spirit body the direct sound-picture-language. It is an all-encompassing transmission that is absolute. For this reason, they do not need to make sure whether the message has arrived and been understood correctly. Because the divine principle "everything in all things" is absolute, there are no doubts.

Every spirit being understands its brothers and sisters, because they are alive in it. Everything is perfect Being, including the language of the spirit beings. The spirit children, the angel children, grow more and more into this all-encom passing Being, into the all-encompassing, detailed communication.

But with people it is different. They often talk about things and situations that they actually do not understand.

The result is the emergence of different meanings, that is, they talk at cross-purposes. This is how misunderstandings arise. As long as people are not in unity among themselves and as long as their neighbor is not alive in their heart, both live in different worlds of thought that keep them from understanding each other.

This is why the human language will continue to be relative until mankind has learned the language of the heart. As a result of this, the words of people will be understood differently from person to person, until the heart speaks. As long as this is not the case, everyone speaks his language according to his consciousness and the world of his thoughts.

This is why the divine revelations are the truth for one person, but for the next person they are untruth. And so, it all depends on the extent to which the individual has developed or darkened his spiritual consciousness, that is, how far his spiritual light of consciousness is able to shine.

In His revelations the Eternal does not take into account the opinions of people. The light of God shines and gives. It gives itself in word and deed. The one who can grasp it and who actualizes the laws of love more and more will attain the expansion of consciousness and will grasp and understand more and more from the treasure of God's love and wisdom. He will then learn the language of the heart and he will know how to read in and behind the words of this world. The one who does not want this can comprehend the revelations of the heavens only in part or not at all. This is why, the following holds true for people, and it is spoken out of the freedom of God: The one who can grasp it may grasp it. The one who wants to leave it may leave it.

Dear brothers and sisters in the earthly garment, what is taught to the spirit children, to the angel children, has already been absorbed by your spiritual body. Everything that lives in infinity, that is, that vibrates, the forces of the eternal All-Being, are opened in you. And so, deep in the innermost part of your soul, you are rich, just as we, the spirit beings in the eternal Being, are infinitely rich. Just as the eternal All-love and wisdom of God is effective in us, in the same way it is alive deep in your souls. After the purification and cleansing of your soul, you, too, will live again in the All-radiation, in the law of God; you will fulfill it and consciously be one with all beings, forms of life and forces. Then, just as we, you will again speak the all-encompassing language, the law of the All. Just as we, you will understand all beings and life forms and you will know how to direct all the forces of the All.

In the eternal Being there are no misunderstandings, for our language, the eternal law, which we are and which penetrates us, is unmistakable. Everything that is reaches unfoldment in and through us. Every impulse that we receive as beings is grasped by us as a picture, as a perfect vision, and every action we carry out is perfect law. We can perceive everything in us; and we create and achieve according to our mentality and our abilities, because we possess the eternal treasure: the seven basic powers of the All.

Every person bears the same treasure in himself, deep in his soul. By explaining your origin and your true being through revelations, we brothers and sisters from the eternal Being are glad to help the person who is willing, who strives toward God and who seriously makes efforts to bring the inner treasure to light.

God's garden of light: the unlimited, eternal law, the radiation network of the All-communication in the unity, God. Sending and receiving

In the eternal Being everything is self-luminous, because the eternal light radiates through all suns and planets, all spirit beings, animals, plants and minerals. Every state of consciousness of minerals, grasses, flowers, plants and animals radiates its light of consciousness. This results in the mighty All-communication—a radiation network that knows no limit. Because everything is in all things and every consciousness is self-luminous, infinity is one great light-garden of God. Through the divine principle of openness and unity, everything radiates, in turn, throughout all things— the smallest, the greatest and the greatest, the smallest. For this reason, in the eternal Being there is no above and below, no right and left, no back and front, no here and there. All spirit beings of the heavens and all life forms in the development planes of the heavens and on the pure spiritual planets form the whole and serve the whole, depending on their state of development, depending on their mentality and their abilities.

All forms of life move in the great light-garden of God and have their existence in God. Those species of minerals, plants and animals, and the nature beings, which are stimulated by the Creator-God, the Spirit of evolution, to develop further, are in a constant evolutionary process, in becoming. The same holds true for the life forms of those plant and animal kingdoms that are found in the gardens of God. When the various life forms of minerals, plants, animals and nature beings are guided by the Creator-God to the next higher step of evolution, they are taken back by the gardens of the eternal Being, by the home planets of the spirit beings, in order to then accomplish the next evolutionary step in the spiritual development planes.

Through the further development of the individual degrees of consciousness, the spiritual dwelling planets do not turn into fallow land. The Spirit of God is movement, creative Being. This is why in the gardens of infinity there is no such thing as standstill. He, the Creator-God, breathes constantly in and out. He lets it become, bringing everything to perfection and stimulating anew to further becoming. Then, in the gardens of the spirit beings, the life forms in the development planes, which develop only very gradually toward the next higher evolutionary form, fill in the space from which the spiritual life forms were taken back in order to develop further.

Everything belongs to the great unity, God. No matter if they are spirit beings or the life forms in the spiritual development planes or in the gardens of God—they are all with one another and for one another and in absolute harmony among one another. They form the great family of God, the Being in the stream of Being.

The law of God is selfless serving. The further developed life forms serve the life that is not yet so far unfolded, and the spirit beings, which are the condensed All-law, serve all Being. They have run through and activated all the degrees of development and are, in God, fully developed Being that has taken on form in the stream of Being. Because their spiritual body, too, was also built up along the same course of evolution and because they have activated all the inherent laws of infinity, they are in constant communication with all the degrees of consciousness and serve all life forms.

For this reason, the life in God is indivisible. The whole of infinity is filled with life and with emerging life forms.

As in heaven, so on Earth

So that it may become on Earth as it is in heaven, I give a revelation on sending and receiving—also in relation to the animal world.

The eternal Being is the eternal law, the All-stream, God, which penetrates everything. The eternal principle of giving and receiving, also called sending and receiving, has effect in Him.

All beings, souls, humans, animals, plants, bushes, trees, minerals, stones and stars live in the All-stream, God, and unceasingly receive the All-stream, the eternal power, God—His love. All components of infinity, even the smallest components of matter, receive the power and the life, God. Every cell of the body, every grain of sand and every dust particle is radiated throughout by the power of God, by the mighty All- stream. And every person—no matter whether he is against or for God—is touched by the All-stream, the eternal energy, God.

God is the giver; He is the eternal law. He, the Mighty, the All-radiation, God, radiates into infinity, and also into matter. All life forms absorb from the eternal law, the All-stream, only as much as corresponds to their state of development. A person, too, can take in from the eternal law only as much as he opens himself to, through the actualization of God's laws. Through actualization the person opens himself to the All-stream, to the law, God, with which he then attains communication. The eternal law gives; it sends. Soul and person receive and send further by fulfilling the will of God. Through this the person enters consciously into the eternal stream, God.

To fulfill the will of God means to repent, to clear up and to no longer commit those negative aspects that a person has recognized in himself.

What is negative? It is enmity, strife, envy, unkindness toward people, animals, toward the world of plants and minerals. The first negative sensations, thoughts, words and actions are the seeds for what then comes into effect: enmity, strife, envy, unkindness, toward people, animals, plants and stones.

To be fulfilled means that whatever a person has actualized fills him with strength, love and wisdom. The one who lives in fulfillment keeps the laws of God. He then lives in the stream, God, and is consciously linked with God. Then he is also united with his brother and his sister and is no longer against them. The result of being one with the neighbor is then also transmitted to the animal, plant and mineral kingdoms—to all forms of life. In this way, the person takes up communication with the positive, divine powers of the All.

People who strive toward God's laws respect their life and that of their second neighbor, as well as the life of the plant and mineral worlds. They will not wantonly kill animals—nor will they slaughter them—and they will not violate the plant and mineral worlds either. Whoever is in the divine communication receives from the All-stream, God, in which he lives and in which all life forms have their existence. Then his spiritual consciousness has immersed into the ocean, God, and is united with the forces of the All, which penetrate him and which he penetrates.

Recognize: Each person can receive from God only as much as he turns toward God, toward the eternal giver.

The pure beings, the spirit beings, receive the total fullness from God, for they live in God's law and are the compressed All-law, God. All other forms of life, like nature beings, animals, plants, minerals and stones, receive light and power from the All-stream, God, all according to their spiritual state of consciousness. What they receive they also radiate, until they, stimulated by the Creator-God, accomplish the next evolutionary step. If the life forms have gained an expansion of consciousness, increased divine energies flow through them. They can then radiate more spiritual energies, that is, give, whichmeans, send. In this way, the spiritual communication builds up very gradually, which is sending and receiving.

According to their particular state of consciousness, all life forms communicate via the eternal law of sending and receiving. Via his matured, light-filled soul, a person can also attain the cosmic-divine communication—when with Christ, his Redeemer, he transforms into light and energy his sinfulness. what burdens his soul and covers up the divine consciousness. Then he, too, attains communication with the divine in all beings and people, in the animals, plants and minerals. He will then perceive his environment accordingly.

The pure sends, in turn, the pure and also receives, in turn, the pure. A person will also receive what he sends, be it divine or un-divine. God, the eternal law, sends. The eternal law does not give way to the human shadows by limiting itself and sending only what is pleasant for the person—even if the person turns away from God. The mighty All-sender, the law, God, is and remains without limit.

God is omnipresent; in Him there is no distance, for He is the All-One and the All-Being which streams through everything.

In this mechanized age, one speaks of transmission ranges. With this he divides wavelengths and frequencies. The broadcasting channels for his radios and televisions or in other transmitting stations have limited ranges. There is no such thing in the eternal Being. As already revealed:

God sends without limit. He, the great All-One, knows neither time nor space. He streams throughout infinity and He also sends in and through the purification planes and to the souls living there. He also sends in and through matter and in and through people. God sends through every little animal, through every plant, through every stone. Every component is penetrated by the All-law, God.

According to the eternal law "everything penetrates all things," all pure life forms penetrate each other. This is why there are no limits for all pure life forms—to which the animals, plants, minerals and stones also belong. For they take in the forces of the All according to their spiritual state of consciousness and send them out again, all according to their state of consciousness.

Minerals and plants are still fixed to a certain location. In the animals, the predispositions for a free will become active. For this reason, animals and, above all, the nature beings, can move freely within the radiation of their consciousness, that is, as far as they radiate. The greater the potential of spiritual particles is, the further the free will radiates in the animals and in the nature beings; their freedom of movement is also according to this.

As far as the radiation of consciousness of the nature beings reaches, they go to the spirit beings and are with the spirit beings, in order to be active with them in the gardens of God. The animals that move inside the gardens of God are also with the spirit beings and the nature beings. According to their state of development, that is, as far as their light of consciousness reaches that they already have developed as light and energy, the animals are in communication with all forms of life and in communication with the spirit beings from whom they are able to take in and understand those impulses that are already developed in themselves.

All life forms send out impulses according to their state of consciousness, that is, they send and receive. The animals—we can also call them children of creation—already sense the names of the spirit beings. When they want to attain a conscious perception with a spirit being, they send out corresponding impulses, in which the name of the spirit being or a life form is discernable to the extent that the state of consciousness of the child of creation is able to grasp it and reproduce it. A mostly matured nature being grasps, with the exception of few details, the full name of the spirit being, because it has built up all cosmic energies in itself, with the exception of a few powers of consciousness.

On the other hand, the spirit beings see and know the respective name of consciousness of the life form. Via this name, they communicate with all forms of life, that is, they speak out and address their names. No life form that is in the process of evolution is addressed by a spirit being as "mineral," "plant" or "animal." The spirit beings call all potentiated forces, all life forms, by their names.

All life forms become independent through the unfoldment of free will. No life form binds itself to a spirit being, even though animals and nature beings with higher degrees of maturity move a great deal with and among the spirit beings. The spirit beings do not bind any life form to themselves either, because they have developed free will that makes them free, that is, independent. The freedom that makes them free also lets their neighbors and second neighbors—that is, the life forms of various degrees of consciousness—live freely.

Invisible helpers on Earth:
Nature beings look after the life forms
of the mineral, plant and animal kingdoms

Dear brothers and sisters in the earthly garment, in my revelation I went back a long way so that you can get an overall view of the development of the life forms and recognize the differences between the conduct of the spirit beings toward the life forms and the conduct of people toward the animal, plant and mineral kingdoms on Earth.

Now I will give a revelation about the patterns of behavior from person to person, from person to animal and from animal to person.

The Earth also carries minerals, plants and animals. The nature beings, which are spiritual and not material and therefore invisible to many people, are active on Earth for all the life forms that still live below their state of consciousness, like minerals, stones, plants and animals.

The nature beings, which cannot be seen with the eyes of human beings and which serve the material nature kingdoms, are subordinate to the spirit beings which, in turn, are in charge of all mineral, plant and animal kingdoms. The nature beings work under their guidance. Via the spiritual forms—for example, of the flowers and animals—they help their material forms. The nature beings work in manifold ways in the animal, plant and mineral kingdoms: They give comfort with their fine, selfless spiritual sensations of consciousness; they radiate the healing and helping forces of the All into the spiritual aspects of animals, plants and minerals; they comfort, protect and built up the material life form as far as it is possible for them. In cooperation with the spirit beings to which the nature kingdoms are subordinated, they form a mighty network of communication that can be compared with a perfectly functioning relief organization.

The eternal Creator set up all of creation on serving and helping, that is, on the communication with all Being. The more developed consciousness serves the yet smaller consciousness, and the smaller consciousness serves the greater consciousness insofar as it can radiate and be active. In this way, the pure spirit beings serve the nature beings and the nature beings serve the spirit beings according to their unfoldment, by together serving and helping the animals, plants and minerals. Just as humans are not alone, so are animals, plants and minerals not left alone either.

Every person, too, has at his side an invisible helper and server, called spirit being or angel being—it is the being which supports and helps him if he, the person, is open to this, that is, approachable. Spirit beings and nature beings serve the animals and plants on Earth as well as the minerals. And so, the animal, plant and mineral kingdoms are included in the serving and helping forces of the spirit beings and nature beings. The angels and nature beings are active invisibly, thus serving people, animals, plants and minerals. They strive to help the spiritual part of the animals and, as far as it is possible for them, also the material body, the envelopment of the spiritual substance.

Animals whose part-souls have not yet been burdened too much by people and animals which still are connected to a collective and have not yet been overly mistreated by people are clairvoyant. They sense, behold and perceive the divine world, the angel beings and nature beings. Especially when animals are in distress, their inner being—the creation- light—radiates more intensely, through which their external form, the shell, the body, is able to perceive the invisible. This then gives comfort and support to the animals of the fields, forests, air and water.

When, for example, animals that live in fields and forests, and now and then animals that live on farms, give birth to their young, they become clairvoyant for a short time and recognize that light- filled helpers carefully radiate light and strength toward them and help them.

Thus, the child of creation feels secure and enveloped in the radiation of the Creator, God, of whom the child of creation, the second neighbor, knows, that He, the infinitely loving Creator-Spirit, is its heartbeat and pulsebeat.

In this way, the Creator-God helps the part-souls and all animals that still are connected to collectives. Suffering plants are also cared for by invisible helpers as much as it is possible for them. The same holds true for the mineral kingdom. The minerals, too, are comforted through radiation and receive the sensation that they are not alone.

How do you, the human, feel
toward the life forms of nature?
Man transmitted his unlawful behavior
to the animals

People are not always the understanding, helpful big brother or the understanding, helpful big sister. Unknowing people have their effect just as they are, that is, unknowing, on minerals, stones, plants and animals. For this reason, the material bodies of the animals and plants correspond to the particular state of development of the life form only to the point where they have not been changed by having been crossed with other life forms.

In the animal and plant worlds, it is like the soul, which is enveloped by a coarse-material shell, the human body. What the soul bears, light or shadow, it radiates, and with this it shapes its physical body. The physical eyes can perceive solely the density, that is, matter. Matter is the envelopment of the spirit, and is therefore relative.

Because man has interfered and is still interfering in the course of life on Earth and of its life forms according to his own ideas, and has therefore changed and is still changing many things, I would like to address my human brothers and sisters with a revelation for which I have chosen the subject: "You, the Animal—You, the Human. Who Has Higher Values?"

Before I can address this issue directly, I ask a serious question of all human brothers and sisters who read my revelation, and with which I want to stimulate an examination into the given facts:

How do humans live on this Earth?

How do many people act toward animals, the second neighbors, toward plants and the mineral world?

Are humans with and for the animal world and for nature and the mineral kingdoms—or are they against them?

Are you, dear brother, dear sister, one with all the substances of the Earth and with all forms of life?

Do you—do many of your fellowmen—have access to the animal, plant and mineral worlds?

Dear sister, dear brother, these questions surely have stimulated your conscience. If they have also awakened your interest for the subject "You, the Animal—You, the Human," then know that my word of revelation refers largely to the animal world; but I will also go into the world of minerals and plants, since they are also life out of the omnipotent life.

Dear reader, think about these questions. Do not say straightaway that you have access to all life forms. Examine yourself!

Do you believe—and in the broader sense, the many people on Earth—that it is in accordance with community life and love for animals, the second neighbors, the animal brothers and sisters, when in apartments and houses animals are kept in cages or, for example, a single cat or a single dog is kept in an apartment or a house? Is this love for animals, when you put your second neighbors, for example, dogs, on chains and give them only little free space to live in or when you keep cats exclusively in your apartments?

Some of you will say: "There is no other way, because there are dogs that need to be chained; otherwise they would attack people!" Again I ask you a direct question: From whom did the animals adopt this characteristic of attacking people?

Do you believe that the spiritual life forms—on Earth called collective- or part- souls—which, as second neighbors, are enveloped in a coarse-material body, have brought these aggressions with them from the heavens? Or has man, over the course of millennia, transmitted this to the animal world through his human, aggressive behavior toward his fellow men and toward the animals?

This influence toward the negative does not show its effect in one single incarnation. This process takes place over the course of many incarnations, for animals that live in a combine of collective souls—including animals with part-souls—also incarnate again and again, until they are called back into the spiritual developmental planes by the Creator-God, the Spirit of evolution.

The innocent animal is chained up because either in previous incarnations or in this present one people have, for instance, hunted and pursued it and maybe even trained it to bite and kill. If for this reason, the animal is not well-disposed toward a person and attacks him, then the person says that it is a wild, fierce beast that needs to be chained up!

I ask another direct question to my human brothers and sisters:

Who is it that would need to be bridled? Shouldn't those people rather bridle themselves or feel the chain who have trained and train their second neighbors to acts of violence or who have acted and act violently against them, thus depriving them of their liberty and freedom of movement?

So-called "dangerous" dogs are put on the leash as a matter of course, so that people are protected from them. But who forced these negative characteristics on the second neighbors so that they became dangerous?

It was and is the people who were and are unkind, hard-hearted and intolerant toward their fellow men, who belittle their fellow men in order to aggrandize themselves, or who berated and berate their neighbors, who made and make them dependent and who brought and bring them up to be yes-men, who trained and train them, so to speak, for their purposes.

People who are not free are trained people, who do as their neighbor wants. By doing so, they have tied their will to the will of the one who oppressed them and trained them to be a yes-man. The one who causes his neighbor to become will-less, contributes to the fact thatannoyance, frustration and aggression build up inside the latter. In many cases, it is the animals, the second neighbors, which have to endure their outbursts.

And so, the danger comes from the human being. He transferred and transfers his dangerousness to the animal. To be fair, the brutal, aggressive, dangerous human ought to be chained or put on a leash so that he come to his senses. In many cases this would be more helpful and salutary, because through this he would be stimulated to change his way of thinking, before the causes he has set break in over him as effects.

One argument used by many people is the following: "We have to protect our second neighbors from the dangers, for example, of fast vehicles, of the clutches of people or of their own unpredictability." Therefore, dogs, for example, have to walk on a leash for several hours, particularly in the cities of this world. Do not say: "Because we love animals, we do it this way. We want to protect them." Is it love to keep, to bring up and train God's creatures according to your criteria and as you see fit?

Is it love to race along your roads in fast vehicles, so that countless creatures of the air are smashed against your cars, against your so-called windshields, or that they are run over and have to thus suffer unimaginably?

Through the negative behavior of people, through the chain, the leash, the cage and through the fact that the second neighbor has to live among people as single animals, many animals became prisoners of those people who have acquired them for selfish reasons and therefore use them accordingly. Many animals are with people only because they are forced into this by them.

Another wrongdoing of people is genetic alterations, the alteration of the predispositions of animals through cross-breeding. Many animal bodies have been crossbred by people so often—thus influencing the genes—that they are unable to live out the natural predispositions acquired from creation, with the result that they hardly have a conscious communication anymore with the Creator-God, the Spirit of evolution. When the part-souls are then called by their Creator, they hardly perceive Him, because they have been deformed, tortured and wantonly killed by many people, or because they ended up in the hands of slaughterers who prepared them for consumption or abused them in experiments.

Humans interfere in the course of procreation by taking the female animal to the male animal and vice versa. And so, humans thus decide if and when the female animal conceives and from which male second neighbor this should happen and in what year.

Whether the species and the predispositions harmonize or not, whether the genes match for the most part, whether the vibration of the blood and the frequency of the bodies fit together, is likewise not taken into account. Whether the law of nature has other intentions with the male as well as with the female second neighbor—despotic man does not ask about that. The animal is to do what the tyrant desires.

If an animal then attacks the despotic person, who once forced it in many ways to do something that was not meant for this animal in the course of the law of nature, then the second neighbor is beaten and tortured because of its improper behavior. In reality, the person received only what he had sown, that is, caused.

For many people, everything that seems to not speak or defend itself is a lifeless, in many cases, a nameless, thing, a commodity, which can be used at human discretion—that is, mistreated.

Dear brothers and sisters in the earthly garment, is this love for the animal world?

Spirit beings and nature beings are untiringly active to protect the collective and part-souls of the animals, in order to maintain the spiritual communication—as far as this is possible—so that they can perceive the call of the All-One when He wants to guide them back into the spiritual development planes.

Pets deformed by human egoism.
Monster man—Slaughterer, violator.
Animal experiments—Senseless suffering

I will now point out another perspective, people's so-called love for animals, the second neighbors, which is nothing more than egoism.

Many animals are kept as so-called lapdogs or treated like stuffed animals, for example, which can be petted at anytime—whenever "Mummy" wishes to—or on whose shoulder Mummy" or "Daddy" has a good cry, or toward which they can think, speak or cry their bitterness, their longings, their spitefulness, their quarrelsomeness and much more, in order to find comfort in the seemingly mute darling. And so, the tears of "Mummy" who cries out of bitterness or self-pity, which are licked off by the pet, give comfort to the pet owner. She thinks that she is not understood like this by anyone else. The result of such deformation is a trivialized, wimpy, sad, spiteful, quarrelsome or aggressive animal that hardly knows anymore its natural creation predispositions and no longer lives them either.

The animal absorbs these aberrations of the human ego. It is programmed by these and becomes deformed. The human aberrations—the deformations of the human ego, which over the course of the ages have formed and shaped and continue to shape the human earthly body—have also shown and show their effects on the animals, primarily on those animal species that live in the immediate or close surroundings of people.

Through this and similar behavior, many pet owners have lost their hold on reality, on the true life of the spiritual planes of Being. It is similar with those animals that are kept by people to serve their purposes and that are used and mistreated to serve the human ego, human passions and human greed, and toward which people think and cry their whole "bag" of thoughts. Through this negative influence of people on the second neighbors or through the false love for animals, a lapdog often takes after its former or present "Mummy" or the hound with its hunting fever takes after its former or present "Daddy."

Where a heart is meant to beat, many people have a nervous stone, which beats solely for their base ego. This is why they can no longer sense and perceive the all-encompassing life—nor that of their immediate neighbor, their pets.

For many people the animal is simply an object without feelings or sensations, which can be tortured, slaughtered and consumed. This is why many animals are kept in a cruel manner, either as production animals—for example, chickens which must lay their eggs—or animals meant for slaughter, so that cannibal man can prepare himself a carcass meal.

Many animals are also kept for research purposes, because scientists are of the opinion that animals do not have any sensations. This attitude relates back to demonic inputs, which aim at disfiguring the creation of the Creator. Among other things, the callused scientists want to get on the track of certain diseases or want to test the effects of newly developed medications on animals—by observing the reactions of the animals. Normally, every person should know that when human beings react, they feel. When animals react, they also feel. Therefore, similarly to people, they feel suffering and pain, as well as fear of an unnatural death.

It is only the fewest of people who know that every disease that can attack the body has its cause within the soul.

Many of the "great men of this world" do not believe in God and His justice because they regard themselves as gods, who, as they think, can manage things as they please.

Through their negative behavior toward the eternal cosmic laws, people became guilty. The guilt is the seed of the guilty one. It entered and enters his soul. The one who has sown and sows receives what he himself has sown into the soil of his soul. At first, the seeds sprout in his soul and then radiate into his physical body. The effect, which can be noticed in the person's body, can be illness, infirmity, blows of fate, loneliness, desolation and much more—depending on what the person has sown. So what can the innocent animal, the second neighbor, do about it, when a person destroys himself through his causes, through his negative seed?

Can animal experiments be of use when the cause of a person's illnesses lies not in his body, but in his soul from where the illness flows out? A medication that has been tested on the body of an animal and found to be good cannot heal the cause in a person's soul. This is why a medicine that is offered by people cannot bring deep-reaching help for the body, because the causes lie in the soul.

A medication can perhaps push an illness back into the soul. This then means a deferment of the illness; however, it does not mean healing, not even when animals had to suffer for it.

The one who knows about the suffering of the animals and remains silent or who condones animal experiments or carries them out will burden his soul accordingly.

As long as animals are slaughtered, parts of their bodies taken from them, their legs and feet amputated, and as long as animals are used for research purposes, humans will be led to the "slaughtering bank" as well, the operating table.

God is unity and life.

For this reason, all animals, plants, minerals and stones must be included in the positive life of the spiritually developing person. A person who changes his attitude to understanding, goodwill and tolerance will find the way to "togetherness" and will gain access to his second neighbor.

The person who respects life will no longer keep animals for slaughter, because these—just as pets—also feel the reason why they are kept on the farm and in the barns. What was and is thought, that is, radiated, toward them by people they absorbed and absorb, for example, when they are ready to be slaughtered. The person thinks about when he might sell the animal to a slaughterhouse or a butcher. He thinks about the sale and already sees the money that he will get for the slaughtered animal. All this comes up in him as pictures. The pictures, which carry all the different frequencies of such thoughts, are either scented or sensed by the animals. The person, who hardly has any communication to life, cannot imagine the fears and distress that comes up in these animals through this.

What the person has and is doing to his second neighbor fell and falls back on him. He will have to endure and suffer the same or similar things. And so, whatever a person has done to his second neighbor, the pets, the animals of the forests, the fields, the animals in the air and the animals in the barns of the farmers or what he has entered into them with his words and feelings, that he has done to himself and input into himself. This is the bitter medicine that he will have to swallow one day.

I have only touched upon the monstrosities that take place in this world and on the Earth with such indescribable cruelty. The person who ridicules or rejects this must ask himself whether, in having such an attitude, he still is a human being, a child of the Eternal, in the image of the eternally loving Father—or whether he is a monster that does not shrink back from anything, that draws everything under his spell, crushing it with his human ego, so that things seem to go well for him. The person who no longer respects anything, except for his human, greedy, passionate, selfish and mania-to-please ego, knows only himself and has to ask himself what state of consciousness he has entered.

A monster consists of brutal, ignoble and vile thought forces. It cannot be compared with an animal, a second neighbor.

The animal, the second neighbor, the child of creation, is the creation from God. It is fine and noble, because the spiritual forms of life are pure.

The human being, too, who lives in concordance with the forces of the nature kingdoms is fine, noble and kind in his thinking and living, also toward his fellow man, because he is in communion with God and gives honor and respect to the life in God. He respects and cherishes all life forms, no matter whether their intelligence is developed in a part-soul through the eternal law that condenses itself, or whether it is still integrated in a collective. He knows that all the forces of life are a part of his true self. He thinks and lives in accordance with this spiritual recognition.

The slaughterer and violator, who thinks solely of himself and has no respect for life, be it human, animal or plant, will have to ask himself—at the latest when the causes break in over him as effects—whether he can still call himself a human being who, according to his origin, is in the image of God, or whether his way of thinking and acting resembles that of a monster that behaves monstrously, that thinks solely of itself, of its own well-being, that treats its fellow man and the animals and plants in a brutal manner and that passes itself off as an idol that is rendered homage and tribute.

The one who does not respect life does not respect his own life either. He rejects it, for he acts against the laws of God. Such a person will have to continue to suffer until his soul has grown through suffering. However, a person who awakens in the Spirit of life and turns back in good time, by following the path of true remorse, of asking for forgiveness and of forgiving, and who no longer does the same or similar things will attain help and find inner peace.

The second neighbor, the animals, as well as the plants and the stones, all of the nature kingdoms, want to serve humans. The one who does not respect and love the life of nature, who does not maintain the communication with the eternal Being, turns into what I have called a monster. The egocentric person disregards the life of his neighbors and second neighbors—animals, plants and minerals—and then wonders when grief, illness and blows of fate hit him. When the life forms pull back from someone who has only bad things in mind, deficiencies appear in his soul as well as in his body. He lacks vitality. The consequences are then illness, need, grief, loneliness, being forsaken and much more.

A time of radical change: A more light-filled Earth with altered plants and animals as a result of the refinement and ennoblement of humans. God regulates the ecological balance through His law of radiation.

The one who attentively observes and senses this world and the people who govern it recognizes that mankind stands in a mighty turn of time, in a gigantic time of radical change. God, the Eternal, spoke and speaks: "I make all things new."

The era of the Spirit rises mightily. Many people are coming to their senses and turning back. They recognize that the old, sinful world cannot be the life. Man is born for something higher than for a life filled with battles, war, torture, murdering and killing. People who believe in higher values and ideals find their way through self-recognition to the motto: Man, you must become divine!

The beginning of higher ethics and morals is the refinement and ennoblement of the person, who overcomes the base aspects that sneak in by way of his world of feelings and thoughts. Ennobled words and deeds rise from his ennobled world of feelings and thoughts. Someone who conquers himself with Christ refines his whole person. The five senses of a person are a part of this. The result of this spiritual unfoldment is the refinement of the whole body structure, and the body also becomes more delicate. Through this gradual change a new person is born.

And so, in the change of times a person becomes more noble and fine, because he lives in more awareness of God. A person of the New Era lives in and with Christ, his Redeemer and divine brother. He gives honor to God in all his thinking, speaking and acting, thus living consciously as a child of God. Through the thinking and living of the new people, the structure of the Earth becomes finer from generation to generation, which means that on a more light-filled Earth the forms and colors of the plants and animals will change.

The era of the Spirit rises mightily and finds an open door in many people, who then orient themselves to God, the eternal law, and become attuned to it. Then what God revealed through the prophet Isaiah about the animals, which one day will live with man in peace and unity, will gradually be fulfilled.

Until the race of God-men is attained, inner guidance is needed. So that a person may reach his innermost being, the God-spark of the soul, the Eternal, His Son and the messengers of God always give people indications—that is, signs pointing the way—so that they can let go of their old patterns and habits, recognize the will of God and fulfill His law. My revelation is also a bridge toward the innermost being, toward the true Being.

The one who listens to the laws of God of his own free will also obliges himself to apply what he has recognized, that is, to actualize it. This is why I now ask those who have read my words the following question: Now that you are a knowing person, how will you behave toward your neighbor—and toward your second neighbors on the farm, in the house, in the barns of the farmers, on the fields, in the forests, in the air and in the waters?

Remember: All animals, no matter whether they are large or small, have organs of perception. No animal may be deliberately hunted, killed and slaughtered.

Nowadays many people are still of the opinion that animals in the forests and fields must be killed, so that the balance, the equilibrium, in nature can be maintained, so that the damage in the fields and forests caused by the food intake of the second neighbor and its like is limited.

Dear brothers and sisters, as long as your souls are damaged, that is, burdened, through wrong thinking and acting, nothing will change in the animal world either.

God's holy order has thought of everything, including order on matter. Do you believe that God needs your guns, traps and poisons to maintain the ecological balance?

God, the All-Spirit, regulates everything through the radiation of His holy order. If humans would not interfere in the ecological balance, God's law of radiation would bring order in the following way: In one animal species, which multiplies too much, for example, fertilization would decrease, automatically as it were. Then there would be less animal young of that species in a certain year or for several years.

God, the Eternal, neither interferes in the ecological balance through killing, nor through the fact that certain animal species take the young of other animal species as prey and consume them. This behavior of animals, too, is again a reflection of humans. Many animals are hunters—but only because men are hunters of prey. It is not the animal that needs to be hunted, punished and killed—man must change his way of thinking and turn toward the laws of God; then the world of animals, plants and minerals will also change toward the positive. Then evil will no longer exist on this Earth, for man will think and live in a divine way.

In this mighty time of radical change, sooner or later every person will be faced with the decision: for or against Christ.

And so, this does not mean: Change your neighbor and your second neighbor. The law says: Change yourself and strive for a positive life that is in the will of God. As you change yourself in a positive sense, in the same way the ballast falls from of the part-souls of many animals, because you, the human being, have cleared up your ballast, your negativity, with Christ, your Redeemer, and with your neighbor as well.

Through the purity of the souls and through the clarity of the part-souls, the external forms, the body structures of people as well as of the animal world will become finer. People who have attained spiritual nobility, that is, whose souls are largely purified, will live with the world of animals, plants and minerals. If people follow the divine laws more and more, then through His power of love and life, the Creator-God will gradually transform in the animal forms the characteristics inflicted on them by man. The life of spiritual people radiates over the whole world of nature and minerals, through which all of the Earth will become purer and its radiation higher. Everything will become lighter and more wide open, because people will have changed toward the better. They are then with God, their Father, and thus with all forms of life.

Then there is peace, and the Kingdom of God is on this Earth.

The great cleansing wave on this Earth.
The human being and his second neighbor
need the contact to the Earth,
to the minerals, plants and animals

The law of sowing and reaping is the wheel of reincarnation, in which the stars have stored and store what humans have caused and cause. The test that will not stop before anyone—be it the authorities of the churches or the state or the scientists or the people—also comes via the law of sowing and reaping. Each one is asked: For or against God?

This great cleansing wave that is set off by the law of sowing and reaping also initiates so-called natural disasters, which are the consequences of the disasters of people: of their behavior, their thinking, speaking and acting. These disasters will take hold of all mankind, since a great part of mankind has sinned against the nature and mineral kingdoms. Everything that is unlawful must be settled and paid off. Then the suffering, the miseries and fears of the animals, the violation of nature and the exploitation of the mineral kingdoms will gradually come to an end, because the slaughterers, the hunters and violators of nature have either converted or been taken away from this Earth.

The thief comes in the night. Therefore, many things will be different overnight. The Earth is still bleeding. She is still being exploited; the stones are crushed by heavy machines, polished and then pressed into shapes that no longer resemble their original state of development. The crushed stones are mixed with building material and are fixed to iron and steel girders, forged to them, so to speak, so that bridges, tunnels and high-rise buildings can be built. The high-rise buildings offer space for many people; for large is the number of souls which want to incarnate again and again, in order to enjoy to the full as human beings what they still carry in their souls from previous incarnations and that binds them to the Earth: ambition, lust for power, greed, the craving for human love and much more.

Dear human brothers and sisters, become aware of how it would be if you were chained up. How would it be if you were kept in prisons? How would it be if you were stacked up on top of each other, like the stones which form the walls and ceilings of the skyscrapers and high-rise buildings?

The person believes that he is a free person. If he looks at his life from the viewpoint of the law of God, he will recognize that figuratively speaking many people are stacked up on top of each other and are tied to each other, and, through sin, are chained up—like the stones that serve them as building material.

The difference between the consciousness of an incarnated and incarcerated soul and the consciousness of the abused stones is that the incarnated soul, the human being, has inflicted and inflicts this restriction onto itself through sin—the consciousness of the stones, however, is forced into them.

Man speaks of the so-called stories of a house. Looking at it from the point of view of a life in the Spirit of God, the heavenly Being, the stories are cells that are stacked next to and on top of each other and are often like cages. They shelter people and animals. Man calls this restriction his home. People live either stacked next to or on top of each other, story by story, either alone or as a family or in a partnership or together with several people—be it in a business, at their place of work or in interest groups. Many of them know each other only by name; in their innermost being they are strangers to each other. For many people their neighbor is "the other one," who is watched from a distance and is checked out in thoughts—"the other one," with whom they are only as much in accord as their thought patterns resemble each other. With mistrust and hostility, they look down on all "other ones" who have different goals and inclinations. These are belittled, called inferior, sized up and weighed, classified accordingly or ignored. The one who has a look into many families of human brothers and sisters or into many an interest group or working group recognizes that many people talk sweetly—but, in their minds, they face each other as enemies.

Someone who has created for himself this image of the "enemy" is of the opinion that he is the best in every respect. Such people think solely of themselves and also love only themselves, thus exalting their base self, their human ego. The person who sees himself in this twilight, which to him is his special brightness, does not think about the law of sowing and reaping; and so, he does not think that the same or similar things could happen to him. Likewise, he disregards the words of truth, which say: Whatever you do not want to be done to you, do not do to others either.

The "other" is also his second neighbor. Plants and stones also live. Plants and stones also feel.

In that cell-like structure which people call an apartment and which is situated on one of the many stories of a house, humans also keep animals.

Recognize: A person and his second neighbor, the animal, need contact to the Earth and to nature, for their physical bodies are nature-bodies, subject to the laws of nature. Through the stories of the building they are more or less lifted off the ground. In time, this causes man and animal to lose contact with the Earth. This lack of contact causes in man and animal apathy, broodiness and in many cases negligent behavior. Consequently, many people hardly respect themselves anymore—not to mention respecting themselves as human beings whose nature is by origin divine. This indifference and passivity also causes their activity at work to suffer, which is then fulfilled in part, in a mediocre way.

The person who has spun himself into his ego-world vegetates. By doing so, he also forgets to take care of himself and of his own needs and to take care of the animal that he has taken into his apartment and its needs. The animal then vegetates in the same dullness and lack of communication as the person does. Through this lethargic, negative behavior, many people have not only forgotten the life with and for their neighbor—they have also dismissed the nature kingdoms from their inner being. Through this many people, animals, plants and minerals became consumer goods, objects, which were and are used, taken advantage of and exploited.

I repeat: Through the egocentricity of people, which is self-centricity, the positive communication with one's fellow man became less and less.

By living in high-rise buildings, in skyscrapers, by living next to, below and on top of each other, man has hermetically sealed himself off from his people and from nature. Through this, the communication with the life of the world of minerals, plants and animals decreased or was sometimes even completely cut off, depending on the person's state of consciousness. From many people's selfishness, from the "me" and the "mine," the mania to dominate arose. Man became a tyrant, who presumed to rule over the nature kingdoms. At the same time, he wanted to subdue the Earth in a cruel manner. This behavior is satanic and not divine.

When the Fall-beings left the paradise of the eternal Being and condensed more and more, the Eternal spoke to them: "Subdue the Earth." This He said out of the law of selfless love.

The law of selfless love is the law of serving, of being for and with one another, of mutual giving and receiving. The Eternal did not speak of exploitation and of brutality toward everyone and everything that lives on the Earth. This non-divine, satanic behavior was prompted by the satanic forces, which are against God, the life. The one who listens to it and follows it is a slave of sin and an adherent of the darkness.

The one who is against God, who surrenders himself in this way to the adverse forces and subjects himself to them is flattered a great deal by them. He receives the corresponding exaltation, until the person, his ego, bends to their will. He is then put to work where the adversary wants him to be.

The New Era—the new life in communion with animals, plants and minerals. The ennobled person in dealing with his animal brothers and sisters

The new man, however, stands in the cosmic Spring of the "Let there be." For more and more people recognize the great deed of the Son of God and are grateful to the Eternal that He guides them and shows them, through messengers of light and through enlightened people, how they should sense, think, live and act at present and in the future, in order to escape the influence of the darkness. The neighbor and the second neighbor, the world of animals, plants and minerals, are a part of the all-encompassing, lawful life. All life forms are in God, for all Being is in God.

Just as the spirit beings are with the nature kingdoms, the people of the New Era will live in a similar way with the animals, plants and minerals. They will understand one another, because they speak one language: the language of selfless love. What the prophets of the Old Covenant have already announced becomes reality. From the darkness of this materialistic world the New Era rises, the Era of Christ, His Kingdom of Peace.

In the Kingdom of Peace of Jesus Christ, what God has announced through the prophet Isaiah will be fulfilled: The wolf will lie with the lamb, the panther with the kid. Calf and lion are friends; they lie together, and children will take care of them. Cow and bear become friends, because in their consciousness there is no longer any meanness, no longer the enmity that was transmitted to them by men. Their young lie together, because their parents also convey to them the peace of men. The lion no longer tears up his neighbor, the animals under him, or even men, because men no longer have carnal desires either, nor crave anymore the consumption of meat. All animals live on grass and straw. The nursing child plays over the hole of the asp; the weaned child puts his hand into the adder's den. Neither the asp nor the adder are hostile toward man, for men and animals have become one, because there is neither fear nor evil and deceit in the human being.

The Earth then carries the life from God, and those who live on it are unified in and with God, because they fulfill the laws of God. All this and much more has already been foretold. God is truth, and His word will come true, even when, seen from the human perspective, many years, even thousands of years, go by.

In the change of time, man will be in communication with the nature kingdoms and thus he will be in communion with all cosmic grades of consciousness.

The one who fulfills the will of God, thus attaining spiritual growth, stands in a friendly and brotherly communion—in communication—with his fellow men and with the nature kingdoms, as well.

Friends and brothers and sisters address each other by name. This also holds true for the second neighbors, the animal brothers and sisters.

As you have heard, all life forms have names that correspond to their respective consciousness. In the eternal Being all life forms address each other by name. The person, who has a name as well, and who wants to be addressed by his name, should also give names to the animals of the house and of the farm and address them with these names. Avoid speaking of the "animal" as such, as often as your language allows this. Someone who has given his second neighbor, his fellow occupant, a name should also use it, that is, he should address his companion by its name.

People who strive to attain spiritual values will ennoble themselves more and more. Through this their manners also become finer. This is apparent not only on the person himself, but also on his surroundings. The unpolished and crude behavior that many people who are oriented to the world still have changes into finer, nobler and selfless behavior. The person feels more deeply and finely, because his spiritual consciousness has become lighter and more radiating. He becomes sensitive, as well.

The sensitive person chooses nobler words, because he himself is ennobled. He behaves accordingly in all situations, also toward his second neighbors, including the plant and mineral worlds. The inner nobility can be noticed in everything that a sensitive person does. He will no longer devour his meals thoughtlessly, for he has learned how to eat, that is, to dine. Then, for him, the second neighbor will no longer "devour," but "eat."

If you truly have learned how to dine and did not simply impose it on yourself as acquired etiquette, which you forget as soon as you are not observed, then you will also get your second neighbor used to eating in a finer way. If it is an inner need for you to eat from a clean and neat dish, which is placed on a clean and neatly laid table, then you will also keep the bowl of your second neighbor clean and put it in a clean and neat spot.

If you are no longer greedy to eat the food, in order to perhaps get the biggest piece, instead eating your meal calmly and consciously, then your second neighbor, as well, will become used to behaving that way. If you do not throw bits of food to the second neighbor, instead placing its meal before it and not trying to take it away again, then it will gradually no longer crave it—that is, wolf it down greedily—but will eat it quietly and peacefully.

If you take care that your place of rest is clean and tidy, then, as a spiritually awakened person, you will also keep your second neighbor's place of rest clean and tidy. Just as you, the order-loving person, air your bed and your bed-covers, so will you do it with the bedcovers of your second neighbor. If you see to it that you regularly wash your blankets and your sheets, then you will also remember that your second neighbor would also like it this way—and you will do this for it.

Just as you have a bed, a niche to sleep in, as it were, so you should also get your second neighbor used to his sleeping-niche. The second neighbor should not sleep right next to you, but should sleep in another room. You can leave the door to the room slightly open, so that he does not feel separated from the others who live there. However, this is not absolutely necessary—not when, for example, two or three second neighbors are together and rest and sleep to-gether; for eventually there should no longer be single ani-mals in the apartments and houses. However, it is important for the second neighbor to have access to the outside.

A neat and clean person cleanses his body daily, brushes and arranges his hair. Remember: Your second neighbor—the dog or the cat you have with you as a fellow occupant—also has a coat of hair. The second neighbor also likes to be brushed and the dog brother or sister likes to be washed now and then. Just as you need to move in fresh air and have oxygen for your body, so it is with your second neigh-bor. It, too, likes to go for a walk and move in fresh air.

The spiritual person knows that all of infinity is based on polarity. Therefore, you, too, dear human brother or sister, love to socialize, and want to have a good boyfriend or girlfriend or a family or people around you with whom you can talk about things.

Remember: Your second neighbor, too, likes to have communication with his kind, for he also has the predisposition for polarity in him, which he radiates according to his state of consciousness and with which he seeks to communicate. Since everything rests on polarity, you also feel that being alone does not correspond to man's nature. People who are alone a great deal and who have to depend on themselves, often become odd, because they lack communication, the exchange of feelings and thoughts.

And so, you do not like to live on your own, without anyone to talk to, separated from your fellow man, alone in a room or in an apartment or in a house, without communication with your neighbor. Your second neighbor as well, which you have taken as your fellow occupant, does not like to live without his kind. You both carry within the same eternal law of love, which is polarity, that is, communication.

If you have taken a second neighbor into your home, then you should know that it likes to communicate with you, the human being, because for it you are a big brother or sister. But at the same time, it wants to be with its kind and likes to communicate with them. For this reason, consider whether you want to follow the spiritual laws and whether you want to take two second neighbors or three or several second neighbors instead of one. Of course, the circumstances need to be considered as well. What helps your second neighbor in developing communication is if one of your friends agrees to take him a couple of times a week to his place, to his second neighbor, and vice versa, so that the degrees of consciousness have their communication, as well. A "place of communication for second neighbors" could also be a good facility, where they are taken care of and looked after in a similar way as, for example, the children in a kindergarten.

However, all these suggestions can bear good fruit only when people change and when they build up a positive communication to their fellow man and to all the forces of life.

In the Kingdom of Peace of Jesus Christ, the second neighbors, the animals, will be with the people. They will not belong to a particular person. It will be a unity and community between people and animal brothers and sisters.

Dear human brother or sister, I repeat an essential point of view. Remember: The second neighbor carries within the consciousness of unity. Therefore, it not only wants to be with you, the human being, but also with its kind. If it has a fellow brother or sister, then it no longer feels alone and lonely and solely dependent on a person. If there are two or three of them, then the longing to meet their kind is no longer as strong, because they can exchange their sensations of consciousness with each another. Then they feel themselves in the great unity, because they can communicate with each another. In time, the result is that they no longer sniff around so much on house corners, blades of grass, trees, bushes, stones and the like. They no longer need to confirm themselves and to search—they have one another. Only the second neighbor who feels lonely searches for his kind. He wants to make himself noticed and therefore marks places with his animal odor, or he wants to sniff his kind. For this purpose house corners, blades of grass, trees, bushes and the like are suitable signposts.

The person who is concerned for his own well-being has dissociated himself from others. He is his own closest neighbor. His brother is "the other one," whom he observes only from without. The person has created his own plot, his house, his land and property, which he watches over and defends. In a broader sense, the world of animals also took on this human behavior. Dogs, cats and other life forms mark their so-called territory with their particular odors. In a figurative sense, man, too, marked and marks his territory with his human ego-vibration, which can also be called his odor.

If, for example, cats had had companions to play with—that is, of their kind—in previous incarnations, then they would not catch as many mice and birds in order to "play" with them so cruelly and torture them.

The behavior of the animals in the wild cannot be taken as a characteristic criterion for their true, original nature. The behavior patterns of the animals in the wild are also determined by what they have absorbed in their part- souls — and possibly also by the aura of the country, the atmospheric pictures of the country and by the magnets created by thought and leadership patterns that are still effective in the countries where the animals live.

What a person emits is also absorbed by the animals. Since no energy is lost, whatever has been radiated by a person will eventually find expression, even if it is only in later generations, in the animal world.

And so, one should not assume that the behavior of the second neighbors in open nature is their true nature and that it corresponds to their particular species and breed. A great deal of what seems to determine the breed and species was transmitted to them by human beings.

The behavior of animals in the wild is often very similar to that of house pets and farm animals, because also the part-souls in those animals that presently live in the wild may once have been incarnated in house pets or farm animals.

Sending and receiving between person and person, between person and second neighbor

Just as a person programs himself with his wanting and desiring, so does he program his second neighbors, the animals.

Programs send and receive. Every brain is a sending and receiving station, including the brain of the second neighbor. The negative programs enter people's souls and also the part-souls of the second neighbors. The difference is that the person burdens himself with this, but with the second neighbor, its nature is changed. For this reason, animals of the same breed or the same state of development often react differently. Many animals also receive telepathically.

Via your technology, for example, via radio and television, many people are stimulated to think. The one who thinks, sends and receives. If, for example, films about animals are broadcast or if people hear in conversations or on radio about animals in far countries or if they inform themselves about animals in other ways, for example, in books, then they, too, begin to think, that is, to send. They will then also receive, in turn.

Every thought is a component of a picture or already contains an entire picture, depending on what is thought. These thought-pictures or elements of thought-pictures are then sent telepathically to the animals that the person has heard about, read about or seen on television. In this way, people influence the animals telepathically; they stimulate in their part-souls what is perhaps still stored in them from previous incarnations. Then the brain cells of the animals absorb, that is, receive, what has been stimulated in them via telepathy. As a result, the animals, in turn, send out what has been activated in them.

Whatever holds true for the communication with one's neighbor, the principle of sending and receiving, also applies, figuratively speaking, to the animal world—and, in its broadest sense, to the world of plants and minerals.

In the pure Being, the divine principle of sending and receiving applies to the spirit beings and to the pure nature kingdoms. The principle of sending and receiving, which has been transformed down on matter in the coarse-material ego-world, applies accordingly in the non- pure, to souls, to human beings, and to the animal, plant and mineral kingdoms that have been violated by man.

Personal sending is human sending; it is telepathy.

Impersonal sending is communication with the pure forces.

A person who is in contact with his second neighbor or with other second neighbors, either via telepathy or via spiritual communication, radiates what he has input into him self. The second neighbor scents this. At the same time the corresponding pictures form in its brain—the same pictures or similar ones to those radiated by the person and which the person had transmitted earlier to the second neighbor. The animal brother or sister then reacts according to these pictures.

If a second neighbor happens to be in a place far away from its hometown and the person it mainly relates to, then a communication band between the second neighbor and this person can be built up through thoughts. When the person it mainly relates to thinks about the animal brother or sister, thus contacting it via telepathy, then those frequencies of this person that have been stored in the brain of the animal as a picture become active. At the same time, this picture also contains the scent of this person, his color and the animal's place of destination and home as a goal.

The dog brother or sister, for example, then sets off; it follows the frequency that has triggered the picture and the scent in its brain. In this way, it again finds its way to its earthly home and the person it mainly relates to. However, the prerequisite is that the animal's brain holds the corresponding programs that have been entered into it by the person or persons it mainly relates to, which then address the animal via telepathy.

What takes place here in a positive, selfless way can also happen in a negative way—through the transformed-down principle of sending and receiving, which can also be described as " stimulating and acting."

Via the transformed-down principle of sending and receiving, a person affects his fellow men, those who have a corresponding receiver, as well as the animals, which, in turn, are correspondingly programmed by people. In its broadest sense, this also holds true for the world of plants and minerals, which has been tortured by man over centuries and which he thus enveloped with his negative energies of thoughts, words and actions. And so, the plant and mineral kingdoms radiate the positive, the divine energies, as well as the negative, the envelopment.

Only when man has changed for the positive, when he has aligned his transmitter to God, the All-power, the eternal law, will everything on this Earth then also change for the positive, for the lawful. That person who has developed the gift to distinguish between good and evil is also responsible for what is happening in this world. For this reason, dear human brothers and sisters, consider: What you feel, think and speak is sending. You will receive the same or like things.

Sending and receiving is not always successful on the human level, neither from person to person nor from person to second neighbor and vice versa. It is similar with our second neighbor as it is with people. It depends on what the person has entered into his soul in previous incarnations. In like manner, this holds true for our second neighbor, the animal: Whatever has been input by people into the second neighbor in former incarnations or in this incarnation is what it radiates.

Thus, the same law is valid for man as well as for the animal world: Like attracts like. Equal and like frequencies attract one another again and again and form a network of communication. Unequal vibrations communicate at certain points of contact or have nothing to say to each other. If different degrees of vibration meet one another, then the person does not understand his neighbor; the animal does not understand the person and the person does not understand the animal. This is why they do not have a conscious communication with one another, even though the divine principle of sending and receiving is always effective in both of them.

The divine principle of sending and receiving eternally sends the seven basic powers into the All. However, people and animals will have a conscious access to the divine All-transmitter only when the person lives an inward life and when the animal has not been deformed by man.

If a person has spiritually awakened, then he will recognize: Just as he treats his fellow man and the world of animals, plants and minerals, so will he, too, be treated. For everything sends and everything that has been sent will have its effect. It is stored and falls back to the sender, according to the causal principle.

The scent-picture.
Communication between a person and his animal brother or sister

The second neighbor radiates the noble, the fine and the good, all according to its spiritual state of consciousness. It wants to maintain the loyalty and connection with people and the cosmic forces.

Just as a person treats his fellow man, so does he treat his second neighbor and all of nature.

The second neighbor perceives you, the person. He sees, hears and smells you, thus perceiving the total impression, which consists of your feeling, thinking, speaking and acting. The total impression is a so-called scent-picture, which the second neighbor retains and enlarges upon, again and again, whenever it meets you anew.

A small qualification must be made with those second neighbors that are still guided by the creation-force via the collectives, which do not yet have a particle composite, or a part-soul. These life forms do not yet have the sensitive, fine and pronounced sensing capacity that a creation-child with a more developed part-soul has. Nevertheless, they sense and feel a person's radiation and his intentions, even if not yet in great detail.

The second neighbors that still live in the composite of a collective are still more withdrawn in themselves. They do not yet have the direct relationship to man, to his reactions and his behavior. They may orient themselves to a person's spiritual radiation, however, they do not yet react externally, or they do so only under certain conditions. On the other hand, the more developed part-souls that have higher degrees of consciousness feel people's sensations and thoughts and their intentions in a very subtle way.

Dear human brothers and sisters, the life forms that are in the process of evolution have spirit bodies in the eternal Being; in the earthly existence they, like people, are enveloped by a coarse-material body. This body can be manipulated by people via thought-energies and via the genes. As you have already read, in order to make it easier for my human brothers and sisters to understand, I call the further developed spiritual life forms part-souls.

Since in those second neighbors with part-souls the basic forces of Will or of Wisdom come to unfold more and more, they react, all according to their state of consciousness, directly or indirectly to their surroundings as well as to people. The larger the particle composite of the part-soul is— that is, the spiritual body—the higher is the state of consciousness of the animal and the greater is the spectrum of its communication possibilities and the further its light of consciousness shines.

These part-souls are already consciously in communication with the spirit beings, and they also want to attain a corresponding communication with human beings, with their spiritually fully developed brothers and sisters.

If people, the big brothers and big sisters, encounter the still developing brothers and sisters of creation with much understanding and good will, then the second neighbors approach them accordingly, as people whom they respect as their big, fully developed brothers and sisters.

In the positive, fully developed human being who is of good will toward them, the second neighbors sense the wisdom of the Creator-God and serve them, according to their state of consciousness. Then people and animal brothers and sisters become friends who understand one another despite their different degrees of maturity. They can rely on each other and are not forsaken. They have a positive communication with each other. Even when they are externally separated for hours or days, they are linked by a feeling of belonging together. This feeling of unity conveys to people in particular the all- encompassing unity of all Being in God.

The second neighbors sense and scent from the sound of the words the present state of their big brother or their big sister. They also react accordingly. They are very sensitive in relation to the disharmony, to the feelings, peculiarities and habits of people.

A person becomes a good observer of his second neighbor when he doesn't live concerned only with himself, but respects in everything the life in God. Such people sense the inner life, the spark of creation, God, in all life forms, no matter how they present themselves at the earthly level. Furthermore, they will respect and cherish all Being more and more. They are true explorers who grasp in full detail the stirrings and movements of the second neighbors and of the plant world and thus learn very gradually the language of the second neighbors and of the plants, and, in a broader sense, also the language of the stones. Because by feeling into the life form, the cosmic communication, the language of the All, builds up in the person.

The second neighbors with well- developed part-souls have a good sense of discernment. They also explore and learn the language of human beings and observe their stirrings. From the sound of their voice, from their choice of words, from the way these are spoken—whether with harshness or kindness, with sadness, despair or with confidence and hope, with selflessness or egocentricity—from this they hear how the person is feeling, whether he is balanced or changeable, whether his nature is sensitive and stable or unpredictable. What they hear and see, they scent at the same time. They scent the smell of the words as well as of the thoughts. For as a person feels, thinks, speaks and acts, that is how he smells. Even tones convey their scents.

An animal attacks—
The cause lies in the person

If a cause comes into effect in a person, the second neighbor scents it before the person notices it. The second neighbor then behaves accordingly. It either gives signals which up to this point were foreign to its nature, or it attacks the person, for instance, when the latter has maltreated it in a previous life or in this earthly existence.

Then the following can happen: The second neighbor has always been a good friend up until now. Suddenly it changes its way of behavior and seems to be unpredictable to the person. The unknowing person beats and flogs it. In reality, the second neighbor had scented from the effect what concerned it—what had been built up between the person and the second neighbor in a previous life or in this earthly existence.

If a person only gives orders to his second neighbor, then it will become a mere recipient of orders. It then does not have the possibility to communicate with its big brother or sister. As a result, the second neighbor withdraws internally, even though, as an animal, it fulfills what the person forces upon it. Over time, tensions arise from this unequal relationship between man and animal. If the second neighbor cannot live out its predispositions, this leads to corresponding discrepancies, which build up in the part-soul of the animal and vent themselves at a given time—when it encounters people with aggressions or when they scare it or drive it into a corner. If this build-up remains in the part-soul, then, in a further incarnation, what I have just mentioned briefly can happen: The animal attacks all of a sudden.

The one who nurtures his human, base ego is of the opinion that everybody must obey him. Such people are deformed, and they also deform the second neighbors, thus preventing a flow of communication between man and animal.

The one who has forced a second neighbor to do something against its will—for example, to chase, hunt and kill other animals—or who chains animals up, acts against the law of nature. What he has caused will fall back on him. Such and similar patterns of behavior are stored in the material stars as well as in the atmospheric chronicle. The deformed predispositions of the second neighbors then call up the same or similar energies from these. Through this, a cycle is formed which causes further negative predispositions and deformations. Through these forces, which again and again radiate to man and animal, many house pets and farm animals, including the animals of the forests, fields and of the great steppes of this Earth and the animals in the air became predators in nature.

May the following questions stimulate you to think about yourselves:

For what reason is a second neighbor with you as a fellow occupant? Hopefully not to help pass the time or for amusement—or even for the purpose of hunting, in order to hunt and kill the animal brothers and sisters of the fields and forests! Whoever keeps animals for this purpose is a kept person himself. He is a driven person, who then vents his aggressions and feelings of discontent in various ways, for example, also by hunting. He then hunts second neighbors with his trained second neighbor, shooting them down and, in his overflowing delight, he takes the killed animal either into his house or sells it straightaway to a slaughterer or, as man calls him, a butcher. From the killed animal, the carcass, pieces of carcass are then prepared, so that he and his like, who also hunt animals or are for killing animals, can have a carcass meal.

The craving to consume meat is also stimulated and increased in those people who hunt, hound, slander, spurn and lead their fellow man to the judicial slaughter bank with negative thoughts, words and actions. Such people know only themselves. They have no inner communication, either with their fellow man or with their second neighbor, the animals. For the egocentric person, only that person is worthy and of importance who thinks and lives as he does. The person who does not blow on the same horn of the human ego will hardly be noticed by a selfish, egocentric person—nor will his second neighbors be noticed, the animals, which are inferior in the eyes of an egoist.

A person transmits his personal thinking and wanting, his limitations, to the whole animal world. At the same time, he acts against himself

Dear human brothers and sisters, those of you who are spiritually awakened and turn away more and more from this satanic activity, give thanks to God, our Father, and Christ, the Redeemer of all souls and men, from the bottom of your hearts, that through their untiring work more and more people find their way to self-recognition and to turn back and strive for a life in God, which is for one's neighbor and second neighbor and for all of nature.

As in heaven, so it shall be similarly on Earth. If people are linked with one another in selfless love, then the animals will also change and again fulfill what is truly their own—the selfless love for and with one another. Then what the Eternal has revealed through Isaiah will happen: Man and animal will become friends.

Many people are of the opinion that dogs and cats neither get on with nor love one another, because their natures are so different. Even though dogs and cats radiate different degrees of consciousness, both still carry the predisposition for unity and communal living. In many cases, dogs and cats do not love each other because they were tied to one person either in a previous incarnation or in the present life and have therefore oriented themselves toward people and taken on their characteristics. When a person lives in disharmony with people, a negative field of tension develops between person and person, a fight, which is carried out in thoughts or with words. This human negative field of tension is absorbed by the second neighbors. They then react in a similar way as people do. From this a fight between rivals emerges. Each wants to have his realm or his certain person for himself. This is true both among the different races as well as among second neighbors who are of the same species.

People who strive toward the All-unity, God, the inner life, feel that infinity dwells in them as strength and light. They think less and less about themselves; they no longer nurture their small, narrow ego, the personal mine and me. They become impersonal, that is, all-conscious.

If a person starts to think in great thoughts, then the second neighbor, for example, the dog and the cat, will change its way of sensing, for in them, too, is the mighty power God, the sensation of the All-consciousness. The one who wants to understand the second neighbors, the animals, first has to strive to understand his neighbor, his fellow man, and to treat him with selfless, understanding love. The largely unburdened second neighbor readily treats his human brothers and sisters with selfless love, for his life, too, is giving and receiving. The second neighbor, the animal, cannot burden itself; it is burdened by people.

The second neighbors, the animals on this Earth, are, like the souls of human beings, enveloped in a material shell. Man and animal can move freely on this Earth only to the extent that the world that has been mechanized by man allows this. I speak about the vehicles, the freeways and roadblocks, various limitations through the mine and me, such as fences, walls and much more. These limitations are felt above all by house pets, for example, dogs who therefore were and are tied up with collars and leashes.

Various species of birds are put into a cage so that they don't fly away; for many of these animal species were taken from other countries with a specific climate and transplanted into a different country with a different climate that

would not be beneficial for them if they were to move freely, for example parakeets, parrots and other exotic animals.
Besides, they should decorate an apartment, no matter
whether it is large or small. If they were to fly freely, then
this would result in too much dirt and disorder for the person who is keeping the animal. But one does not ask whether the warm, dry air of the rooms where people live agrees
with the little animal or not. The human motto is: "Adapt
and delight me."

Hamsters in their little houses are made to believe that
when they move along inside a turning wheel they are run-
ning along their familiar path—the distance that they want
to run daily in order to stay active. This is the human being
and his motto. But whether the animals loose their orien-
tation in doing so is not questioned.

Rabbits are put into hutches to give people pleasure.
Then, at so-called holy feasts like, for instance, Christmas
or Easter, the dear friends are slaughtered and eaten. The
motto of the person is: "Serve me, even to the point of tast-
ing and eating you."

Deer are kept in game preserves. They endure similar
things as the animals in barns and in the forests and fields.
The motto of humans is: "Whatever can be eaten will be
slaughtered."

Fish are kept as decoration in apartments and gardens to
delight the people living there. In your restaurants and ho-
tels, fish are placed into tanks from which customers can
pick out a specific fish, which is then killed and presented
for consumption. Few become aware of why the fish again
and again swim along the edges or glass walls of the tank.
The fish, for instance, the ones called goldfish and trout, are
deceived by the reflection of the water coming from the
edge of the tank or by the glass of the aquarium. They believe that the water in the small pond or aquarium they live

in continues; deeper waters surely have to come, in which they could find the nourishment that they need for the growth of their bodies. Their bodies need different substances every day, not the food that is put before them by people, what they are fed, which people call fish-food.

All animals live, like people, in a rhythm of day and night. However, each day and each night have different rhythms, depending on the constellation of the stars and planets and depending on what these radiate toward the Earth, toward human beings, animals, plants and minerals. For this reason, a person, as well as an animal, needs that nourishment which these rhythms stimulate in him on this day via the taste nerves and the sensory organs. This applies, above all, to people and animals and, in a broader sense, also to the world of plants. Plants, too, have their daily rhythms.

According to the law "like attracts like," a person is stimulated via the taste nerves and the sensory organs to take in specific substances for nourishment on this day. His taste nerves and sensory organs establish communication with the plants and the different kinds of vegetables that the body needson this day and which radiate rhythms that are similar to the ones the individual person radiates today.

This is why, it is said: Do not worry about tomorrow. Live consciously today and do not worry about the morrow; then, even today, you will be guided into the tomorrow, and you will sense in time what you should think, speak, do and eat tomorrow. This does not mean that one should not make a plan for his days and weeks. Planning means guidance. A person who does not act upon the plan in a controlling way, but who lives consciously and lets himself be guided by the plan, will do what is important today. And the one who cultivates his land for tomorrow will also take from the field tomorrow those plants and vegetables that radiate toward him today because of his own radiation.

A person transmits his own limitation, his personal thinking and wanting to all of the animal world.

All animals, no matter which state of consciousness they have, are in the Creator-God, in His law of development, and they have their existence in Him.

I repeat: The one who acts against animals, plants, minerals and stones acts at the same time against himself. His spiritual body is the All that has taken on form; to this also belongs the spiritual essence of the animals, plants, minerals and stones.

A person who violates the forms of life brings the same suffering to himself, for he sins against the life, and thus, against himself.

The eternal law says: Whoever respects his neighbors, his fellow men, and the nature kingdoms lives with the forces of nature, because he consciously has accepted them and absorbed them. Solely through this will he attain perfection as person and soul. For the life is a great whole, the unity in God. Since everything is in all things, the soul of the person and the person himself are called upon to again unfold, within himself, the divine that is in all things.

The negative enters the part-soul of the animal as a memory—It enters the soul of the tyrant person as a burden. The causes are coming into effect

Dear brothers and sisters, the one who has made a decision for the inner life, for God, is for his neighbor and his second neighbor. You have read that the life forms perceive their surrounding and everything that approaches them, all according to their state of consciousness. In the behavior of the person they can scent and sense what he intends to do, which means for them guns, knives, daggers, scalpels and much more. Even if the person outwardly behaves as though he would not harm the animal, the animals scent the thoughts of people, for these, too, have their odor.

Second neighbors will behave at present and in the future according to what radiates toward them. When you meet second neighbors or when you visit them in their barns, remember: They, too, have eyes to see with. They, too, have ears to hear with. They, too, have a mouth to talk with. Even though for people the language of the animals is merely sounds that are not understood by many, they still tell of what they scent and sense. Many voices of the animals are of such fine frequencies that a human ear is not capable of perceiving them. A person regards the life forms of the animal, plant and mineral kingdoms as mute—and yet all of creation talks. A person who is for his second neighbor also understands their body language, their gestures, which is many times clearer and more direct than the language of sound.

Every animal, no matter how inconspicuous it may be, has sensory organs and organs of perception, with which it registers its environment and its human brothers and sisters, as well. The organs of sensing and perception of many animals have become dulled, particularly those of house pets and farm animals, because many people work off their aggressions on them. The result is that the animals are unfriendly and intimidated where human beings are concerned.

A person who wants to live with animals must first of all live in peace with his fellow man and be largely well-balanced, in his inner being as well as externally. A person who wants to sense into and recognize the world of animals, plants and minerals must first recognize himself and overcome and clear up the "un-divine." Only then, will he attain the right view and through this, insight into the life of all life forms and the inner sensation and feeling for the whole of nature.

It is not the second neighbor, the animal, that needs to change, but first of all the person who has changed and deformed the second neighbor, the animal. Only that person can build up a positive communication to his fellow man and to the animals who has purified himself through self-recognition and by clearing up his negativity to a point where he can first recognize himself in every situation.

Every person wants to be taken into consideration.

For a person it goes without saying that his fellow men address him when they request something or when they want to invite him or when he should be present at a conversation or the like. You say: "It goes without saying that I first ask and request something of my fellow man and that I not just grab his arm and pull him along. For what I do not want to be done to me, this I will not do to my neighbor either." What would a person say if he were to be grabbed and pulled along by another person without explanation or if he were to be roughly woken up, grabbed and without a single word or only with the word "come on!" be torn out of his sleep and dragged along? Some people would perhaps use the word "barbarian," which means: You uncivilized, cruel, uncultured, brutish person! Just this statement shows what goes on inside a person who is treated by his neighbor in this or a similar way.

How is our second neighbor treated? The despotic human kicks the second neighbor, for example, the dog, with his foot and yells: "Come on!" Where to? The despotic human does not need to tell this to the creature that he regards as inferior. It is to obey and serve him. The animal, the second neighbor, crawls tiredly and seemingly mute after the person. Possibly it will be even put on a leash and pulled along—where to?

What the "barbarian" wants, the animal can often no longer scent—either because it has been deadened or because it has been programmed by people in such a way that it merely follows the "must" of the tyrant apathetically and intimidated.

The same is true for housecats. They are disturbed in their sleep because the person wants to pet them, or they are roughly pushed off the chair where they lie and are sleeping.

The bird in the cage is woken up or activated in some other way with signs, for example, through whistling or words—just as the person wants it.

The hamster's behavior is disturbed—because the person just wants it that way.

The turtle is picked up and brought to some other place it didn't want to go to at all—merely because that person wants it that way.

The rabbit is taken out of its hutch and carried in one's arms. Whether it wants this or not, whether it wants to absorb the person's present vibrations is not asked. The animal is meant to obey. The animals in the barns are taken out, turned out to graze or hitched to the carriage—whether they want this or not. With them the rhythm of resting and being awake and active is not considered either.

Do you, the person, want to be treated in this way?

Countless animals had and have to bow down before tyrannical man, because the violent human being enslaved and enslaves them with his might and his satanic powers. Through obstinate commands, with blows and cruel measures, the animals were and are brought to heel.

The second neighbor has to submit to all of this, for it is the weaker one and subjugates itself to the tyrant person. However, the person, the tyrant, cannot change the sensations and perceptions that the second neighbor stores in his part-soul as pictures.

Everything an animal experiences, be it good or not so good, enters its part-soul as a memory, not as its burden; yet it is burdening. On the other hand, the negative behavior of humans toward their fellow man and toward animals, as well as toward the world of plants and minerals, enters their souls as a burden. So a person can force many things onto his second neighbor, thus covering up its spiritual predispositions and changing its physical predispositions. However, he cannot extinguish anything.

According to the law of sowing and reaping, everything comes to light, also the offences against the world of animals, plants and minerals. One day, perhaps not until another incarnation, the animal will encounter its tyrant and will then behave accordingly, all depending on what the person, whose soul is in an earthly garment once more, had once done to the second neighbor.

These encounters do not happen by chance, as nothing in the whole cosmos happens by chance; instead, the great causal computer, the law of cause and effect, brings them about. When the causes come into effect, they often become active in this incarnation under quite different circumstances and conditions. The former tyrant, the human being, and the formerly enslaved second neighbor encounter each other. The memories of the part-soul in the second neighbor are the former scented pictures, with which the animal now scents the soul in that person who once tortured, flogged, beat and perhaps cruelly killed it—for even burdens have their specific odor. And so, the vibrations collide, and from the radiation of the person the animal scents the former tyrant, the hunter, the beater and the like—and it scents what this person once did to it.

If an encounter is not possible on the physical plane, then the law of cause and effect becomes effective in the spheres of purification—or the soul has to expiate as a human being in a further incarnation what it once did in another earthly garment to the nature kingdoms, without having, for example, to directly encounter the second neighbor that was abused by the person.

Young animals at a turbulent and impetuous age: The human being— A good example for his second neighbor. Advice on nutrition, a daily routine

The second neighbors, too, have their period of turbulence and impetuosity, similar to human children.

During this time, the second neighbors know very well what they should do—but they do not always do it. In the young animals there is a little imp, in a positive sense, that often urges them to do something that should not be done. This little imp develops with their growth spurts. Just before a growth spurt, the young animals are calmer; they are in a waiting phase. When their growth spurt is past, they feel increased energy. They want to show this increased energy to themselves and to their big human brothers and sisters. It is similar to a child; when it has learned to ride a bicycle, then it wants to show to itself and to its parents how big and strong it is and how it can keep its balance. But often things go wrong. For example, the second neighbor will suddenly get a shoe and tear it to pieces or rip up a garment or bite some other thing to pieces or it will ignore the call of its big human brother or sister who wants to call it back to his or her side. And so, the little energy-imp cuts capers.

So, bring up the second neighbor that you have taken to yourself with much patience, for it has to first find its way in this world and form its scent pictures.

The world-oriented person who is woven into his own world thinks that his measure is the right one. However, if he looks into this world and observes the violated nature kingdoms with open eyes, then he must recognize that what takes place in the world and in nature is a mirror of his cast of mind, of his standards. One recognizes the perpetrator by his deeds, by his fruit.

Whatever man sows he will reap. This is true on a small as well as on a large scale. It holds true for humans and for the second neighbor. Whatever the big brother or sister can get away with, so will the little brother or sister, the second neighbor; for the person transmits his standards to animals, plants and minerals, to the nature kingdoms. For this reason, it does little good if the person, for example, tries to instill in the second neighbor to be good and self- possessed toward people, that it should not scratch or bite them, or, for example, bark loudly at another dog brother or sister. If the person is an example to it for scratching, barking and biting, then the second neighbor will become neither good nor self-possessed.

It is similar with eating. If a person never learned to dine, then the second neighbor will wolf down its food. If a person eats a great amount of meat, then the dog brother or sister will also want a corresponding amount of meat. If the person cannot curb and ennoble himself, then he will not be able to curb and ennoble his second neighbor either.

The following advice is for those human brothers and sisters who have second neighbors living with them:

During the animal's puberty, it is not recommended to give them raw meat as their main nourishment. A small piece every now and then is not harmful for the second neighbor that is being programmed correspondingly by the person; fanaticism should not be applied.

Generally one can say that substances in raw meat have an effect on the hormones stirred up during puberty, and provoke an over-excitability in the second neighbor.

It is similar with a young person in puberty. He craves meat or strong drinks or cigarettes or drugs—when he has stored the same or similar things in his soul, and also when his problems become too big. If the young person does not have a good role model and if he was not brought up to be disciplined and consistent and to have the right inner and outer bearing, then he often just lets the days slip by—without any great interest in a specific task that he can carry out in a consistent and concentrated manner. Such a person then breaks out of the social norms and reacts like the second neighbor: He scratches, bites, rants and raves.

For this reason, one's own standards must be looked at, that is, how the individual person himself thinks, speaks and acts, what his deeds are—before wanting to raise human beings or animals.

The food that is fed to the second neighbor should be given in moderate amounts; however, no slimming cures should be carried out, as people do in a way that is contrary to the laws of nature. The second neighbor should be offered an amount of food that does not overstrain its digestive organs and body. In the morning, at noon and in the evening, it should receive enough to make it satisfied, but not full. The portion should be adjusted to the size of the second neighbor and its activity. In its dish put only as much food as is meant for this meal. If it does not want to eat right then, it can eat later. Between meals, restorative substances or gifts of love are not inappropriate. The dog brothers and sisters can also be given a bone now and then, for its substances are conducive to the growth of their body. However, the second neighbor should not be spoiled.

Decisive for everything is that the person or persons whom the animal relates to are of a mostly even temperament, because the person transmits everything that he is to the second neighbor. Especially during puberty, when the second neighbor cannot quite cope with its body, it absorbs people's vibrations very sensitively, particularly those of the people who care for it. It takes in the positive as well as the negative, and also the peculiarities of the person.

A person should always judge his second neighbor by his own standards. What he does not want to have done to himself he should not do to his fellow man or the animals either. This also holds true concerning sleep. When you are in deep sleep, you do not want to be roughly roused and urged on, because you feel that this shock is not good for your nervous system. The same is true for the second neighbor. Do not rouse them when they are sleeping; by doing so, you are merely driving them on and stirring up their nervous system.

If they are supposed to get up because you intend to do something and plan to take them with you, then wake them up gently and behave in the way already revealed.

If they can sleep, do not disturb them. Especially the young second neighbors in puberty still need a regular daily routine. Long walks should be made only after they have had a good sleep. Always start from yourself: What applies to human beings should, figuratively speaking, also apply to the second neighbor. When you are tired and should then go for a long walk—how do you react? Your second neighbor reacts similarly—aggressively! Normally, a time of rest should be planned for people around noon. This holds true for the second neighbor, as well.

The one who recognizes the second neighbor as a part of himself will feel into the respective situation of the animal brother or sister. For example, when he wants to take the sleeping second neighbor, the dog, with him, because there is no other possibility, then he will first stroke gently several times over its coat. As soon as the second neighbor moves, he will tell it in a calm voice, using pictorial words, what his lawful intentions are, thus giving it an idea of where he is going and to where the second neighbor should accompany him and what will be done there.

Whenever you address the animal brothers and sisters, link your words with a picture, in which the course of action is shown pictorially. The second neighbor, for example, the dog brother or sister, then scents the pictorial words. From this a scent picture then develops for the second neighbor, to which it then orients itself. It will gladly get up then and accompany its big fellow brother or sister.

The sound-picture input of messages to the animal brother or sister

Whatever the second neighbor takes in, that is, what he scents, becomes a picture in him at the same time. Speak to your second neighbor as you do to your small children. Always say in advance what you want to do, for example "Now we are going shopping" or "We are going to visit someone" or "There are visitors coming" or "We are going for a drive in the fields or into the forest" or " Stay alone now for some time."

No matter what you say, at the same time develop this into a picture that you input in the second neighbor.

Tell it, for example, that you are going shopping and that it may accompany you. Show it a picture of the way you will take, what it is like. In mental images, show it the shops that you will go to and at the same time input a picture of how it should behave in the shops. The same is true when you expect visitors: Input in it a picture of who is coming—woman, man, child or the whole family—and the general behavior of the visitors.

If you intend to take the second neighbor with you in a vehicle, then at the same time input a picture of what the vehicle looks like, where you will drive to and who you may meet. And when you take your second neighbor into the open fields or into the woods, input a picture of whether you will be walking or using a vehicle. Tell it this in sound and picture, that is, describe it in sound-picture-language, including what will be done in the field or forest.

No matter what you convey to your second neighbor—it should go into it at the same time as sound-picture-language, for your words as well as aspects of the pictures have their scent. From this, the scent picture develops for your second neighbor. Whether it absorbs the sound-picture-language, which aspects it grasps and which ones remain in the dark for it, depends above all on the state of development of its part-soul and, beside this, on what the part-soul had experienced in its earlier incarnations.

A person who respects his neighbor and himself as a child of God will also accept and receive his second neighbor as a creature of the Creator. Then he will put the second neighbor, for example, the dog, on a leash or tie it up only when there is danger.

Whatever house pet or farm animal it may be, respect its free will and do not intrude into its temple, the spiritual life of your second neighbor, in which it also moves. Be with it in a continuously positive communication, and by the second neighbor's stirrings you will feel and recognize how it wants to feel and live.

And when your second neighbor does not sleep, no matter what you plan to do with it, enter this into it in pictorial words. The second neighbor should sit when you tell it what you intend to do, unless it has just woken up and is still lying there calmly, but alertly. You can also tell it what you are planning while it is still in this position. Both intensify its attentiveness. Input your plans c a l m l y.

And when the second neighbor should stay home, tell it this calmly and tell it where you will go, that you will come back and that it is now its task to watch over the house, the farm or the apartment. Bring it a small gift as a reward now and then, something which tastes particularly good to it. Stroke its coat and praise it for its watchfulness and understanding.

Consider: The second neighbor is a part of you. Being a second neighbor in the house or on the farm, it does not want to follow you around either. Nor does it want to simply go along with you; it wants to walk with you, if possible next to its big brother or big sister, perhaps in front or for a short while behind you. For it still has the characteristics bred into it by people, that is, the predispositions of the corresponding breed and the inputs made by man. Accordingly, it also reacts to its surroundings.

Feeding the second neighbor.
Craving meat—
A programming from previous incarnations

Dear brothers and sisters, feed your second neighbors, whom you have taken as fellow occupants into your homes or apartments, the way you should feed yourselves. Take care that they receive all the trace elements and vitamins that your body needs, too.

Before you eat, you should give food to your second neighbors, or give them their food at the same time you have your meal. And so, the food of the second neighbors should not differ too widely from what you eat. A lawful life, also in relation to food, holds true for humans as well as for the animal brother or sister.

Nature gives you and your second neighbors everything that the nature-body, including the shell of the soul or of the part-soul, needs. Often the second neighbor still wants to have meat. Give it the amount that is good for it, perhaps once, twice or three times a week. Here, too, it all depends on what kind of food your second neighbor received in previous incarnations. Everything is based on vibration, and so it is possible that what the senses of smell and taste once absorbed can still radiate from the part-soul or be in the genes, for example, the craving for meat. The radiation of the part-soul or of the genes also have their effect on the sense organs of the second neighbor, so that it then craves meat. You have heard that what the soul brings with it from previous incarnations marks the body. This also holds true for the part-soul of the second neighbor. So show some understanding here, too.

Recognize, for example, that if during a previous incarnation a second neighbor was raised to be a hunting dog or if the animal received large amounts of meat to eat or if it formerly lived with people who raised animals for slaughter or slaughtered them itself or if an animal lived near a slaughterhouse or butcher shop, then the little part-soul still carries in it the scent-picture of suffering, of melancholy and of the consumption of meat. And so, never be fanatical, neither with yourself nor with your neighbor and second neighbor, for you do not know which predispositions still lie in the soul of the person or in the part-soul of the animal or in the genes, which become active at a given time.

In people as well as in the second neighbor, a ravenous hunger and the craving for meat should not be suppressed, but directed into the right channels. The desire or the craving for meat should be reduced very gradually in people, as well as in the second neighbor. For the person, it is important that he change his way of thinking, that he ennoble his sensations and thoughts, through which his feelings and senses refine. In this way, the right perception and attitude toward the neighbor and the second neighbor also grow, so that the person senses and feels more, and then acts accordingly. Then the meat and fish portions gradually become smaller and the intervals between meals with meat and fish become longer. In this way, the old program, the craving for meat, phases out. At the same time, a nobler and finer program develops, which perceives the subtle forces, the gifts of nature, so that the person then chooses his food accordingly. The person then no longer smells of consumed meat, to which many animals have oriented themselves through scenting. The person, whose senses have become finer, will then also behave accordingly toward the world of animals, plants and minerals.

Recognize that everything on Earth, the good, the not so good or the vile, derives from human beings. A help to readjust the organism can also be the use of appropriate seasoning. In the transition stage from meat and fish to natural food, the meals for you as well as for your second neighbor can still be seasoned somewhat more strongly, until your sense organs and those of the second neighbor have completely reoriented themselves.

The right measure in all things—in people as well as in the second neighbor—gradually leads to the unfoldment of the spiritual forces of the soul. The one who readjusts his organism and that of his second neighbor in a lawful way will not lack anything. Steamed vegetables, raw vegetables or grains and fruits, everything prepared in the right way, contain everything that a nature-body needs.

A person who overstrains his nerves and those of his second neighbor needs to additionally provide his body with vitamins, trace elements and the like.

And so, it is similar with the animal as it is with humans: Just as the person should gradually turn toward nature and all that nature offers him, he should do so with the second neighbor he has taken to live with him.

So never be fanatical, for fanaticism, too, is a state that comes from facets of the human ego.

Display patterns of the animal—
Copied from humans.
The second neighbor scents the world of
sensations and thoughts of human beings

Realize that the person who only seems to be vegetarian merely wants to show- off, because he can show only few spiritual-divine qualities. Then he adopts a rule of life that has not grown from within and that will not make him a spiritual vegetarian, either. A spiritual vegetarian is a person who has outgrown the consumption of meat and fish through his spiritual development, because his world of feelings, thoughts and senses has become finer, because he follows the basic ethical-moral principles of life.

The animal—the second neighbor—however, is uncomplicated. It does not have predispositions like, for instance, exalting or belittling its neighbor or the like. The second neighbor does not need this; for it is linked with nature and respects the Creator-power that streams in it—unless humans have deformed it by having violently interfered and by still interfering with its earthly life and by having trained it to be a poacher, a robber and marauder of nature.

What the second neighbor has copied from humans is their display behavior. With this it wants to ingratiate itself, so that the person is good to it. At the same time, it wants to show what it can do. And the "Give your paw" or "Sit up and beg" or making itself noticed by scratching and pawing with the foot—which is supposed to mean "Please, please" and other things—was transmitted to it by people.

So be earnest and straightforward with the second neighbors. With their pure sensations they see you as their big light-brother or their big light-sister. When you have become aware of your cosmic existence, then you will also behave accordingly toward all people and the nature kingdoms.

Do speak with all house pets and farm animals, no matter which state of consciousness they have. And when you serve them their meals or feed the farm animals, tell them what kind of food it is they are receiving from you, and when feeding them, remember they also need what nature gives to people and animals, according to the season. Address them as their big brothers and sisters. They will understand you according to their state of consciousness. In this way, what God revealed through Isaiah will be fulfilled: And the animals will be friends to man, because man is to the second neighbor brother, sister and friend.

Therefore, respect your animal brothers and sisters, the second neighbors, for they wish to be true friends to you. Strive to treat them as you would like to be treated. Then you will soon learn to understand them, and they will be in positive communication with you. Always remember what is essential: He who wants to have a peaceful environment must first become peaceful himself. This is true, above all, for the human being, because he is the one who has sown the lack of peace.

The following sentence is part of the law of development for this Earth. It holds true for the present and the future:

If you want to live in peace with your neighbor, including with the animals, plants and minerals, even with the whole Earth, then you must first become peaceful, yourself.

A person who strives toward this principle will become understanding and gradually attain a fine ability to empathize, and the recognition and perception that all life forms sense and perceive according to their spiritual degree of development.

The whole of infinity consists of color, form, sound and fragrance.

The adversary of God took this holy principle, reversed it and applied it in a contrary sense: He related and relates it to the base human ego and transmitted this via humans to the animal world. By doing so, he drew down the forces of the All in order to establish his territory.

Since the whole of infinity is based on color, form, sound and fragrance, all pure life forms—the ones in the heavenly pure worlds—radiate their fragrance of unfoldment, that is, their fragrance of consciousness. These are the finest, absolute, divine vibrations.

The spirit beings, too, emit their fragrance. It corresponds to their mentality and their abilities. All heavenly fragrances, sounds, colors and forms come together in the mighty primordial stream, God.

Every burdened soul emits its fragrance, all according to its burdens. Every person has a different body odor, which corresponds, in turn, to the light-filled or the burdened soul. The same holds true for all forms of nature, including the part-souls. All of them radiate the fragrance of creation, the forces of creation, all according to their state of development and their spiritual predispositions.

What they have adopted from humans—and here I think of house pets in particular—also has a fragrance or an odor.

I repeat some statements, so that they may be impressed upon people's minds. The following lawful principle is also a repetition: The second neighbors register the person anew, over and over again. Every time a person meets an animal, he will be scented again or perceived most exactly, because every person has at every moment a different radiation, a different fragrance, which he emits. For all his feelings, thoughts, words and actions have an odor. At every moment a person also makes different movements, which, again, are controlled by his world of feelings and thoughts. The second neighbor perceives this as well.

Watch yourself and your second neighbor: If you live together with a second neighbor, for example, with a dog brother or sister, in an apartment or in a house, every time it encounters you, it will scent you over and over again, in order to grasp you the way you are at the moment, according to your world of feelings and thoughts. Every second neighbor grasps people according to its state of consciousness.

Everything is energy, so is food, medications and beverages. A person smells according to what food, drink and medication he consumes. The animal brothers and sisters in the houses and on the farms, in turn, scent this—and in the broadest sense, so do the animals in the woods and fields, when a person walks through the woods or across the open fields. The same holds true for his world of feelings and thoughts and for everything he does.

The second neighbors register everything about the persons who are directly around them, and in the broadest sense, they also scent what people think and speak and put into the atmosphere, which then, like the radiation of the sun, again radiates down on people and animals. A person absorbs it according to his correspondences. The animals absorb it, because they have been marked by man in past generations and in this incarnation. It shapes their world of senses. They then act toward people accordingly, specifically and generally. The second neighbors take on impulses from people that their consciousness is able to register, because they want to serve people, or guide them, depending on their programming, depending on what has been input into them by people or what has been forced upon them through punishment.

A person can pretend before his fellow man and act as if he were understanding and tolerant—but not before the second neighbors, especially not before animals with correspondingly developed part- souls.

People who are linked with nature and develop the awareness that everything lives and that everything is contained in all things will also attain again the spiritual gift of positive communication with the life, the Being. The Being is the life, in all spirit beings, in human beings, souls, animals, plants, minerals and in the stones. It is the Spirit of the All.

A *lawful input of life-programs for the second neighbor*

Animals are not individualists; they are beings with different states of consciousness and differing experiences with people. For this reason, a person who wants to live with animals also needs to learn to understand their language and their behavior. He will not attain this by studying the behavior patterns of animals with his intellect, but by developing in himself the divine aspects of the worlds of animals, plants and minerals through a life according to God's laws—that is, if he returns to his impersonal being which lives in God. As a result of the shadowing of the part-souls caused by humans, the second neighbors in houses and apartments need to be cared for differently than farm animals or those of the fields and forests.

When a human being sees the light of day, that is, when a child is born, then the soul has to make its body "practicable." The child learns to stand up, to sit, to walk, to talk. Its parents or those people who are around the child help it in this. The small child also needs to take in its life programs for this Earth, for the behavior and communication among and with people.

It is also similar with our second neighbors, the house pets that live closely together with people. The same words and expressions should be used on them over and over again, until they grasp what is meant. This is why the person who, for example, has taken in a dog brother or sister as a fellow occupant should input into it the words and expressions that the second neighbor needs for a life on the Earth.

They are words that give the second neighbor an understanding of lawful behavior patterns like "sit," "go," "back," or "be careful," or "it's ok"—when there is no danger—or, when there is danger, "watch it, danger" or "attention, road," "attention, vehicle." Over and over again, the same words and terms should be input into the second neighbor as pictures.

According to their spiritual state of development, all animals in coarse-material bodies also have brain cells. Animals with part-souls, which show varying degrees of development, also have a corresponding brain mass. Animals with a greater potential of particles took and take in what people radiate more quickly and in more detail.

However, all animals speak their own language—whether they still are linked to a collective or whether they already have a part-soul. Every animal, including the microorganisms that are invisible to man, have their language, their communication. Be it the animals in the air, in the waters, the animals on or in the Earth—they are all in communication with each other and with the All and have their language, all according to their state of consciousness.

For this reason, it is of little use to study certain animal species, for most of them adapt, as far as it is possible, to the conditions of their environment. Their behavior patterns in the air, on and in the Earth and in the waters, no longer correspond in most cases to their inner spiritual clock, to lawful processes. They adapt, as already revealed, to the conditions of their environment and in many cases absorb what people force onto them unlawfully or brutally or what people enter into the atmospheric chronicle through their way of thinking and living—which then, in turn, has its effect on people, animals and the environment.

For this reason, the same holds true again and again: Man, develop yourself toward the higher, lawful powers;

and you will create the corresponding living space for yourself and also for the world of animals, plants and minerals, in which you and the animal world can live lawfully. Figuratively speaking, this holds true for the world of plants and minerals, as well.

So that the animals that live among people—for example, dog and cat brothers and sisters, and also farm animal brothers and sisters—are able to understand according to their consciousness, to understand the living habits of human beings and their thinking and doing, their brain needs to be programmed with lawful programs for life, as with human children.

As already revealed, the words that are input as pictures and which form into programs are gradually absorbed by the animal's brain mass. In this, the tone of voice is also decisive. The words should always have the same intonation, that is, the same sound.

When there is danger ahead, the words should be spoken with emphasis, so that the second neighbor senses and scents exactly what is meant by it. However, it should never be expressed in a commanding tone.

Treat your second neighbor as a good friend that trusts you and learns to attain communication with its big human brother or sister.

Do consider well which ideas you input into your second neighbor. It should never be against the law of God, for example, the law of nature, but solely and exclusively what is necessary for the protection of man and animal.

I repeat: The one who inputs his hunting fever into his second neighbor will one day himself be hunted. The one who chained it up will one day himself be bound. The one who kicks it will one day himself be kicked. The one who beats it will one day himself be beaten, and the one who trains it to attack people will also be injured, attacked and treated accordingly one day by one or several animals. The one who slaughters animals will one day end up on the operating table himself, and the one who uses animals for experimental purposes will one day himself become an object of dark forces. All unlawful patterns of behavior and pictorial inputs will direct themselves against man.

And so, the person who violates the law of God, of which the laws of nature are also a part, will have to endure corresponding things. Commands and pictures of coercion are against the law of nature, for the second neighbor, too, is entitled to be treated with the right amount of respect and freedom. The person who keeps this law will attain unity with the second neighbors, yes, with all of nature.

In no case should one ask too much of a second neighbor. For example, what a dog brother or sister is meant to do should correspond to its breed and its state of consciousness. According to its state of consciousness, each dog breed brings with it corresponding predispositions and abilities. An alert person linked with God, who is one with the nature kingdoms, will choose a breed that corresponds to his mentality, to the meaning he has given to his life and to his living space, and he will support the predispositions and abilities of his second neighbor.

Not every animal reacts to the inputs of a human being. Many second neighbors react unnaturally, because orders to hunt, to kill and to destroy were entered into them in previous existences. And the trivialization of animals, as well as the torturing and suffering when an animal is slaughtered or when it had to serve as an experimental object—all these things enter the part-soul of the animal and radiate out again from it. It reacts accordingly.

All life forms that have been culpably altered by humans must be led back to their original state of development by them. The divine world advises and teaches

Repetitions of what has already been revealed are necessary in order to deepen it.

Become aware of the following once again:

Through the frequent crossbreeding of animals with differing predispositions and through the interference of man in their world of sensations and perceptions, a highly developed part-soul can dwell in a small, stocky and ungainly animal body, for example. On the other hand, a part-soul that is still several steps back on the scale of development can dwell in a large and imposing animal. Through crossbreeding, an influence was and is exercised on the genes of the animals, so that various kinds of body forms emerged and emerge, which, in turn, have corresponding predispositions. This is why, in a small, perhaps stocky animal body, can dwell a part-soul that is highly developed on the scale of evolution, a part-soul that may stand shortly before its unfoldment into a nature being. And so, not every animal body corresponds to the level of development of its part-soul.

These excesses of the human ego, which lie in the crossbreeding of animals, and all other similarly inventive ideas became and become a burden for man.

Through his unlawful behavior toward the nature kingdoms, man has created causes upon causes. All causes must be paid off, no matter whether they concern one's neighbor, the second neighbor or the whole of nature.

All the guilt that mankind has loaded upon itself via alterations, control or encroachment upon the life forms must be expiated by mankind, for all life forms must be brought back to their original state of development. So that this may happen on the Earth again in many ways, the divine world gives advice and teachings again and again.

In the Kingdom of Peace of Jesus Christ, the animals will be with the people, and the animals, plants and minerals will serve them consciously.

May my words, which I have revealed through a human mouth, through the instrument of God, be fulfilled soon. Then there will be peace among men, and the animals will be people's friends. They will live with them and the people will live with the animals. People will be for and with their neighbors and their second neighbors, and the second neighbors will be with and for people, who are their big brothers and sisters. This will be, for God has revealed it.

In the Spirit of the Almighty, the new heaven and the new Earth already exist. This radiation-picture of salvation will accomplish on Earth what already is in God. I, too, Liobani, behold the new heaven and the new Earth for the people in the Kingdom of Peace of Jesus Christ.

Peace

Appendix

More Books:

This Is My Word
A and Ω
The Gospel of Jesus

The Christ-Revelation that true Christians
all over the world meanwhile have come to know

Jesus of Nazareth stood up for the animals. Would you like to know what Christ says today concerning the destruction of the environment, animal experiments, life and death, illness and healing? Read *This Is My Word*, a book that is auspicious and shaking in its message; it is given in the clear prophetic language of the Spirit of God. Much that is missing from the Bible or has been passed on ambiguously is clarified in this book. The reader learns about basic spiritual correlations that enable him to better understand and master his life. He discovers Jesus of Nazareth as the Son of God who did not bring the people an external religion, but God as the kind Father of love—a God who does not punish or seek revenge, instead loving His children infinitely and showing them the path, so that they may find their way to a free and fulfilled life in God.

From the Table of Contents: There is no punishing God – God is unlimited love and freedom – The birth of Jesus – the Fall- event – Pharisees yesterday and today – Equality of man and woman – Every person is a temple of God – Explanation of the miracle of the food – Dying out of many animal species – About the nature of God – and much more.

We will gladly send you a free booklet of excerpts from this book (36 pages).

1078 pp., hardbd., Order No. S 007 en, US$ 19.99, ISBN 1-890841-17-X
Also available in German, Spanish, French, Italian, Russian, Polish, Croatian, Serbian, Slovenian

Healing by Faith –
The Holistic Healing

A book that brings home to everyone what is really important in life. It helps the reader become aware of the value of his life on Earth. It contains detailed explanations of the relationship between illness, or health, and our own way of living. It brings GOD home to us as the source of power in the innermost being of every person.

From the Table of Contents: Our body of itself cannot become ill – Original Christian healing by faith means to activate the faith in Christ, by making use of one's day – The source of power, GOD, can do everything – An exercise to see on ourselves how our feelings and thoughts affect our breathing – The word "incurable" excludes hope – and much more.

104 pp., Order No. S 330 en, US$ 6.99, ISBN 1-890841-10-2

What You Think and Say, How You Dine and What You Eat, Shows Who You Are

We receive hints and help to shape our life on a higher level. We learn to know and understand ourselves better and we are given the tools to draw closer to our true being be recognizing ourselves and clearing up the negative aspects we find in ourselves.

110 pp. Order No. S 135 en, US$ 5.99, ISBN 1-890841-02-1

Ten Little Black Boys

What Bamba experiences as he awakens to the inner life, as he learns to pay attention to the voice of the heart and to listen to it alone, as he sets out with nine other black youth to bring the commandments of God to his fellow man—all this says much to the one who has an open heart for the mighty Spirit of life, God. (for children and adults)

74 pp. 10 colored ill., Order No. S 610en, US$ 5.99, ISBN 1-890841-03-X

The Prophet

The voice of the heart, the eternal truth,
the eternal law of God,
given by the prophetess of God for our time
The fundamental issues of our time
to think about and to serve in self-recognition

... Free

The Prophet

The voice of the heart, the voice of truth...

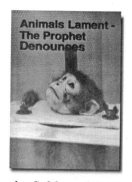

Animals Lament – The Prophet Denounces

The assumption of humans that takes for granted the right to rule over animals and people with cruelty – where does this come from? Is there a method to this madness?

The Prophet lends a voice to the animals and exposes the roots of our disdain of them. *"Why do you cook, fry and cut up our body? Did the Creator not give you the herbs and the fruits of the fields and forests? What have we done to you that you keep us in prisons and feed us your waste products? Your hearts are poor in feeling and merciless. ... Learn to be compassionate by putting yourselves in our position..."*

Order your free copy: The Prophet No. 15

The Murder of Animals Is the Death of Humans

Did we humans really believe there would be no consequences for the centuries of exploitation, plunder and now pollution of our dwelling planet, the Mother Earth? And what about the disdain, torture and slaughter of God's creatures, the animals, in the cruelest ways possible? We have deluded ourselves because now: The cup is full! It is enough! After all the cruelties humans have inflicted upon the animals and nature, they are now on the line. What this means is shown uncompromisingly and clearly in this booklet. And who is behind this destructive activity? Who is a part of it? Everyone is free to take the shaking words of the prophet to heart and change something – or believe he has nothing to do with it. But the following holds: "It is as it is. Nothing will change this, whether we believe it or not."

Order your free copy: The Prophet No. 16

All the editions of "The Prophet" listed on the previous page are available free of charge, as well as our complete catalog of books and cassettes. Contact:

Verlag DAS Wort GmbH
Max-Braun-Str. 2
97828 Marktheidenfeld
GERMANY
Tel. + 49-9391-504-135
Fax + 49-9391-504-133

The WORD
The UNIVERSAL SPIRIT
PO Box 3549
Woodbridge, CT 06525
USA
Tel. 1-800-846-2691
Tel. 203-882-1549
Fax 203-457-9396

Universal Life
The Inner Religion
PO Box 55133
1800 Sheppard Ave. East
Toronto, ONT M2J 5A0
CANADA
Tel. 1-800-806-9997
Fax 416-487-6396

Gabriele Publishing House
P.O. Box 2221, Deering, NH 03244   n
(844) 576-0937
WhatsApp/Messenger: +49 151 1883 8742
www.Gabriele-Publishing-House.com